PRACTICAL DISCIPLESHIP:
A UNITED STATES CHRISTOLOGY

J. J. Mueller, S.J.

A Michael Glazier Book

THE LITURGICAL PRESS
Collegeville, Minnesota

A Michael Glazier Book published by The Liturgical Press

Cover design by David Manahan, O.S.B.

Cover icon by Charles Rohrbacher

| 1 | 2 | 3 | 4 | 5 | 6 | 7 | 8 | 9 |

Library of Congress Cataloging-in-Publication Data

Mueller, J. J. (John J.)
   Practical discipleship : a United States Christology / J.J. Mueller.
      p.   cm.
   "A Michael Glazier book."
   Includes bibliographical references.
   ISBN 0-8146-5012-0
   1. Jesus Christ—Person and offices. 2. Christian life—Catholic authors.   I. Title.
BT202.M78 1992
232'.0973—dc20
                                  91-38571
                                      CIP

CONTENTS

PRACTICAL DISCIPLESHIP:
A UNITED STATES CHRISTOLOGY

PREFACE

The origin of the word "faith" in Hebrew experience means to lean on someone with all one's weight. It is an action word that describes the way we live. Christian faith begins in faith, not doctrine; in practice, not theory; in encounter, not ideas. When Jesus asks his disciples, "Who do you say that I am?" it comes in the middle of the Gospel. We can easily forget that the disciples have already been following Jesus for some time. The most important line addressed to them until now has been Jesus' first invitation: "Come follow me." If they had not followed, Jesus could not have asked his question. The disciples had walked with Jesus, witnessed his miracles, experienced his compassion for the poor, heard him preach the kingdom of God, watched that kingdom break into their midst. All these experiences brought them to the possibility of acknowledging the truth of Jesus: "You are the Christ."

This book on Christology examines the act of following Jesus as the cause, not the consequence, of proclaiming him. Most people learn from their experiences and instinctively trust them, even when they conflict with elaborately formulated ideas. So in this Christology we will begin with practical discipleship as a basis for reflection.

I operate on the principle that theology belongs to the people of the Church, not to theologians or Church officials or musty tomes handed down. We need to recapture what is rightfully the possession of everyone. Granted, the truth claimed by any individual or group must be tested by the wider people of God and its tradition. But we are in need of a vital, honest, integral, and challenging theology. There is only one purpose for theology: to bring us closer to God.

Let us accept the reality of two thousand years of Christian encounter with Jesus, and enter this conversation in the middle of an already existing love affair. The experience is similar to being born into a family. Each of us experiences life as brand new, as if it began with us. We need not reject the long and varied story that preceded us. To accept the responsibilities of today is our challenge.

To be responsible is to accept the contextual dimensions of our belief. One such dimension is the social one in which we live—namely, the United States of America. The Jesus Event never lets us reduce our experience to culture, but it does call us through and beyond that culture to the God who sustains us.

To do a Christology for the United States is, therefore, to be faithful in response to God's fidelity. The incarnation implies that God has entered into this world in a new way and extends throughout it for the purpose of saving us. Concern for social and cultural affairs is a concern for everyone's salvation. We accept responsibility for one another, both at home and globally. The task of theology is to articulate where God is calling us and how we should respond, and to put this message at the disposal of others in the Church in the context of the gospel.

In Latin America, Africa, India, the Philippines, and other parts of the world, theologians are examining the cultural and social implications of following Jesus. They are asking Americans to add their own experience to the global conversation. The time to speak has arrived. We need to articulate who we are and why we act the way we do. If we have a vision that includes others, then we must present it and let others criticize it. As the most powerful nation on the globe, we must say what responsibilities we have and what we hope to see happen.

This book would not have been possible without two recently extended opportunities to learn from other cultures. I am indebted to the Jesuits and many people of the Philippines who took me in and raised more questions than gave answers to the U.S. culture and to the Jesuits in South Africa and the Oblate seminary of St. Joseph's in Cedara whose faculty and students constantly pushed me to examine the U.S. context for doing theology.

The Jesuits are a marvelous group and the many Jesuits from all over the world whom I have spent countless hours talking with and learning from are a vital part of this book. For over ten years

I have been part of an ongoing think tank on American philosophy and theology called the John Courtney Murray Group that has been an important contribution to this book. Therefore I want to thank Don Gelpi, Frank Oppenheim, Bill Spohn, John Stacer, Stephen Rowntree, Carl Starkloff, John Staudenmaier, Drew Christiansen and Mike Mahon for their invaluable insights and suggestions.

It is not unusual that students share both an important part of teaching and the shaping of teachers. I especially want to thank the many students at St. Louis University who have raised the questions and provided solutions that sensitized me to the need for an academic presentation that I address in this book. I want to thank my colleagues in the theology department at St. Louis University who have encouraged me to pursue this work. Also, the manuscript has been thoroughly enhanced by the editorial suggestions of Jeanette Batz whose sensitive and wise judgments contributed to the work.

And finally, I want to thank several important conversation partners in my family with whom I have conversed about this project for many hours: my sister Cathy, my brother Steve and his wife Mary, all of whom have dedicated themselves to the gospel in the U.S. context. Their discipleship remains a constant source of nourishment and insight for me.

INTRODUCTION

Five men were arguing about the meaning of life. After long heated hours of discussion they were unable to resolve their differences. Each person was unwilling to yield what he experienced as true. Then a wise guru joined them, and offered to shed whatever light he could on the problem, if they wished. The impasse was knotted so tightly that the five agreed; each one secretly believed that his position would be proven true.

The guru took the five men and blindfolded them. Then he brought an elephant into their midst. The five had never seen an elephant before. One he directed to the ear, another to the leg, the third to the tusk, another to the side, and the fifth to the tail. The five blindfolded men examined the elephant. The guru then asked them, "Well, what is an elephant?"

The first felt the ear and said, "An elephant is like a large leaf in a tree, swaying in the breeze."

Feeling the leg, the second took exception to this and said, "You are right that an elephant is like a tree but not the leaf. It is like the sturdy, hard trunk of a tree as round as a man's arms."

The third man affirmed the second but, while stroking the tusk, corrected him saying, "Yes, hard but not like a stump. It is smooth, curved, and pointed like a branch made of stone."

Rubbing the elephant's side, the fourth interjected, "No, it is more like a wall with texture. It is wider and softer than any of you realize."

Shaking his head, the fifth man could only contradict such silliness: "No. You all are wrong. An elephant is like a rope, supple yet frayed at the end, and held easily in one hand."

The guru, gently stroking his beard, smiled knowingly and asked the men to remove their blindfolds. Then he said to the five astonished men, "Who is right?"

"We all are," they exclaimed.

He smiled again and replied, "Yes, you all were right—and you all were wrong. Life is the same. Each one of you knows it from your own experience—all that you believe is true, but all of it is incomplete."

This story reminds us that in the pursuit of the whole truth, at best we possess only a slice. It follows that when we articulate truth we do so from one perspective. Many other perspectives, or articulations, exist. Of these, some are better than others.

In writing a Christology, one feels like one of these five—not so much wise as fervent seekers of truth. I cannot help but reflect that, if an elephant is this difficult to get hold of, imagine what it would be like to handle the developing, living reality of God and the Church. Then add to the five's challenge the possibility of knowing the elephant from its minute biological dimension as well, the flowing of blood, the cells growing and dying, or the various sensations, or know sight itself and the mystery of hearing. To "touch" the God-human encounter in Jesus is a truth beyond even that.

The word Christology is a theological word used to designate the study and understanding of Jesus the Christ. Most importantly, it is not an independent area of study but extremely relational, and central to Christianity. It is Jesus who tells us who God is for us, and who we are before God and one another. Christology has a historical content that, like the elephant, we can put our hands on: the titles and images of Jesus down through the ages and testifying persons, whether eyewitnesses, later saints, or theologians. Christology also has a personal, present truth that is a living encounter with Jesus Christ today. Every Christian shares in this living reality. Because we follow this living truth, we are disciples and, since Antioch in the first century, have been designated by the name "Christians."

In Christology, a tension exists between knowing more and more about the past and living a practical discipleship in the present. Some theologians describe this tension as one between academic and pastoral concerns. In my judgment this tension reflects the highly relational character of Christology and is therefore a helpful tension, one I would not wish to resolve. The reason for this is that we know a great deal about Jesus through his life, death, and resurrection, the eyewitness testimony to his message, and the subsequent living of that message down through the ages by other disciples like ourselves in different contexts and cultures. Emerging from this two thousand year history is a continuing and purifying grasp of what the Christian message entails.

Knowledge about Christ is never an end in itself but a means to help us follow Christ in our lives; going to heaven does not require passing a Christology exam but, rather, it requires us to feed the hungry, clothe the naked, give drink to the thirsty. Every age provides new challenges and invites new responses. When we accept these responsibilities, we do so in accordance with the demands of Christian discipleship. Like a man or woman in a marriage, we encounter life's demands from the strength of our committed relationship. The bottom line for Christians is that we seek to transform our lives and all that we do into a loving act that brings us closer to Jesus, God, and one another. Christians call it the Great Commandment: love of God and love of neighbor.

Since the 1960s, Scripture scholarship has placed a tremendous number of new insights at our disposal. This wealth of scriptural studies might be considered the greatest theological achievement of this century. Christology has benefitted from this scholarship, turning to the well of Scripture to drink deeply.

At the same time, since the 1960s tremendous societal and cultural developments have taken place. For example, economically we no longer live in an Industrial Age but in an Information Age. In philosophy we have moved from Enlightenment values based on the concept of an individual's autonomous reason to post-enlightenment values based on the concept of a related self. The organism model as an approach to the study of all things human, a product of nineteenth century evolutionary thought, has been replaced by an interpersonal model. Our age is changing and expanding its relationships at the fastest pace in human history. New challenges present themselves every day.

Given our growing knowledge of Scripture coupled with our fast-moving world of increasing linkages, the area of Christology that needs attention is bringing the Scripture and the world together in a living discipleship. The purpose of this book is to examine this living discipleship.

To enter into a living discipleship is to recognize the responsibilities that life presents to us. This is a process of discernment, wisdom, and prudence mixed with prophecy. Clearly one way that discipleship requires Christians to respond is through involvement in society. Much of who we are comes from the strengths and weaknesses of our society. Freedom, opportunity, ways of acting, support, security, defense, and survival are the reasons for, and responsibilities of, the collection of people called a society. This society also presents images of success and failure, models of what it means to be male and female, and values about what is right and wrong. The societal images, models, and values may or may not be those of a Christian disciple. If they are, the disciple can support them. If they are not, then the disciple must resist them. Either way, the disciple is an active contributor to the making of that society.

This Christology seeks to examine what the United States society challenges the disciple to be. It is an American Christology in the sense that the primary societal environment taken into consideration is the United States. We who live here have been shaped by that environment, both consciously and unconsciously.

One potential problem with a United States Christology is that it can become too narrow. Every culture supports a system of truth, including ways of verifying it. But by thinking it has the total truth and not a partial one, any nation can become self-serving. The nation claims a truth with which other nations may disagree. One nation believes it is right; another is just as sure it is wrong. The nation claiming that it holds the truth may have the power to enforce its views. Every week in the newspapers we have examples of this: from Iran, the former USSR, Nicaragua, South Africa, Japan, China, and Europe, to the United States. In 1989, 40 countries were at war. It is reckoned that 80 verifiable wars have occurred since 1945, and, depending upon the conditions used to classify a war, that number could be as high as 145. Thus the danger is real for a narrow nationalism to become an ideology which only wants to win.

That a narrow nationalism can occur in the consideration of a Christology is a danger we must take steps to overcome. What will prevent this sort of nationalism? There must be a commitment to a reality beyond the nation. Through that commitment we can call any nation's excess to judgment, and applaud all good efforts. A negative idea such as mutual self-destruction, which is built on fear and named "deterrence," should be rejected as adequate. A positive idea which translates into a goal and a good is a better option. The commitment is one that works for the good of humanity as a whole. Of course, what constitutes humanity must be more clearly stated, but without the openness and willingness to put the good of humanity above the good of one nation, narrowness and self-serving nationalism will reign. So, while our purpose is a United States Christology, its scope is the wider global humanity.

No matter how wide our scope, however, we experience humanity most directly in dealing with the responsibilities of our family, our friends, as well as our social, economic, and political realities. These begin at home and come back to roost at home. A United States Christology is not opposed to a worldwide theology; quite the opposite. It seeks to be even more responsible to everyone by recognizing its own strengths and weaknesses. By clarifying its partial grasp of truth, it can enter into the wider process of truth. Truth is pursued together, and the more people know themselves, their motives, and their limits, the greater the possibility of finding the truth in a wider context.

Only with this wider concern for truth in mind can anyone suggest an examination of a particular Christology. Just as all people differ, so do nations: in history, resources, people, culture, education, accepted ways of doing things, child rearing, participation in society, and so on. To find the invitation of Christ in these particularities is to accept the truly incarnational aspect of our discipleship. Likewise, to ignore these particularities is to ignore God's incarnation in our lives.

This book is about discipleship. Its concern is living the Christian life within the context of the United States' society. Its scope is not, however, limited to people of the United States. This Christology is but one more voice within the human community in pursuit of a responsible faith, now and in the future. Latin American, African, Indian, and Oriental cultures are investigating how they can be responsible within their historical context, and the United States cannot stay out of this worldwide discussion.

Discipleship means following Jesus. Within theology, Christology is the area which examines the context by which we articulate and measure our following. Therefore it is with Christology that we begin.

The book is divided into three parts. The first part examines the terms of Christology and the United States context. The second part takes eight constitutive themes of Jesus' message. Each theme is explained scripturally and then considered in a United States context. The variety of possible responses is infinite but the pattern is the same: each suggestion asks us to see *what we are responsible for* in our particular context. A series of questions at the end of each section is meant to help the reader study alone or discuss with others in a group, in order to clarify his or her discipleship. The third part examines a theology of discipleship through the two organizing themes of spirituality and practical response. Its purpose is to systematize our thinking about committed action, and to identify aids and dangers in judging a practical discipleship.[1]

It is my conviction that the gospel question to Peter, "Who do you say that I am?" might very well be the most important question about Jesus' identity, but it is not the most important moment of discipleship. That moment comes in the form of Jesus' first invitation to Peter: "Come follow me." Only if we, like Peter, follow Jesus as disciples can we freely come to profess what we have learned by following Jesus: "Yes, you are the Christ." As the Gospels indicate, following Jesus is the way we come to profess him as Lord. How we find, encounter, and follow Jesus as disciples in our situation in the United States is the subject of this book. Thus it begins, not in Scripture but in the practical experience

[1]In terms of Bernard Lonergan's theological method, "practical discipleship" belongs to the eighth functional specialty—*Communications;* and it comes from the seventh functional specialty of Systematics. Cf. *Method in Theology* (New York: Herder and Herder, 1972) 335–369. According to David Tracy's theological method, "practical discipleship" belongs to the third area of Practical Theology, and it comes from the second area of Systematic theology. Cf. *Blessed Rage for Order* (New York: The Seabury Press, 1979) 237–50.

of Jesus as Lord. The intent is for us to learn more about Jesus, profess him, and thereby live practice and profession together in discipleship.[2]

[2]Edward Schillebeeckx has presented systematic theology with a model for working between two areas—scriptural and systematic—in his *Jesus* (New York: The Seabury Press, 1979) and *Christ* (New York: The Seabury Press, 1980) volumes. This book does the same; however, it moves from systematic to practical theology, i.e., taking the reflected upon faith experience from the scripture through tradition in order to see what implications it has for a lived discipleship.

Part I
The Context

WHAT IS CHRISTOLOGY?

Christology is the study of Jesus of Nazareth who is the Christ, the anointed one of God, who lived, suffered, died for our salvation, was raised from the dead, and sits at the right hand of the Father in power and glory. The Holy Spirit of the Father and the Christ continues to abide with us in the transformation of the world to God. In simple terms, Christology is the study of the "Jesus Event" in all its dimensions.

The sources for the study of the Jesus Event are (1) the eyewitnesses of his life, death, and resurrection; (2) the earliest disciples who shared their relationship and understanding of Jesus in an oral tradition; (3) the liturgical testimony, especially the sacraments; (4) the written testimony that became the canon of the New Testament, especially the four Gospels; (5) the continuing tradition in the lives of communities, in both a written and non-written form; (6) the many attestations in Church documents, theological writings, lives of saints, art, and architecture; and (7) the continually present experience of the living, believing community. It is that experience in all its variety which becomes the tradition.

The first six sources above mainly deal with the investigation of the past as it illuminates the present. The past is not blindly brought forward and applied to the present, but retrieved according to two criteria: our present situation and the past situation. For example, we can only read the Gospel of Mark from our present situation but, in order to be faithful to our tradition, we also must know what the Gospel of Mark intended for its own time. We must know, according to textual criticism, what Mark's reli-

21

gious, social, and historical contexts were, and how his words were received by believers. We need the general critical skills of interpretation called literary, historical, social, and scientific criticisms.

The seventh source, the continually present experience of the living, believing community in all its variety, is fluid rather than fixed, welcoming rather than retiring, dynamic rather than static. The Christ experience is happening now and, therefore, is more difficult to capture in clarity and force. Life is messy: mistakes are made, poor choices and good choices go indistinguishably side by side, and only the hindsight of history provides the perspective upon whatever lasting effects prevail.

Because this seventh source is shifting daily and occurring in many places through many people, it is the least clear and must rely on the beacons of directive and corrective sources for illumination. Nevertheless the living tradition is discipleship in the making, and is thereby the most important source of all. It is Christology based upon a living discipleship in the following of Jesus. As such, it is the subject of this book.

To live as a disciple today requires a double investigation: we must explore both the Christian message and the situation within which we live. The Christian message, which we can also call "tradition," "Christian witness," or *kerygma,* is always received by us at least partially in a historical and societal context. There is no disembodied Christian message, as the Jesus Event itself declares. We know that all revelations of God have come in a particular time and place, and have depended upon the receptivity of human persons who articulated what God spoke. Today is no exception.

Now let us look a little closer at our situation. Any investigation of our situation cannot be removed from how we follow Jesus. We are not first century people belonging to a semitic race, coming from a Jewish tradition, living under Roman occupation. We are twentieth century people, from one of many different races, living in an already-shaped Christian tradition, in an American context. It is here that we follow Jesus.

One does not, however, enter into this situation with a blank slate. We enter with a knowledge of the Jesus Event and how it invites us into discipleship. For example, in the religious experience that may have developed out of our family and personal experiences, the role of love is central. That Christian kind of love, and not other kinds of love that are seen on television or heard in songs, is a central part of our situation and remains part and parcel of all Christian discipleship. Thus, one of the most practical steps we can take in our discipleship is to learn about Jesus, what he preached, who he was, what he did, what he revealed about God, to what he called us, and how others have lived that discipleship down through the ages. These steps are addressed by the first six sources.

The Christian message cannot be blindly applied to any set of circumstances. And our current circumstances do not easily accommodate the Christian message. The solution is a critical analysis of both the Christian message and the lived situation; they must be fitted together, with a critical correlation of the data. Once that is done, the Christian message may either support or reject the values found in the present situation. Whichever happens, the consequences become a guide for living discipleship.

"The situation" is not simply the immediate, visible reality. Today, primarily through a heightened social awareness, we know that invisible factors with far-reaching consequences influence us. In the broadest terms, these factors are those of culture and society.

Vatican II (1962–65) was the first Council to use the word "culture" as a theological construct *(Gaudium et Spes)*. Since then, theologians have paid attention to culture and its diversity in many forms. This is no easy task, because we are dealing with every human dimension (such as language, silence, movement, rest, birth, death, action, values, stories, learning, roles, religion).

Perhaps the clearest advocates of attention to culture have been the theologians from South America, Africa, and India. Their initial reliance upon European thought did not match the experience of their people, and so they took a bold new step in the analysis of their social, cultural, political, religious, and symbolic roots.

Church documents, especially *Evangelii Nuntiandi* (1973), have continued this line of thought and added a new method for examining ways of living the Christian message in different cultures. *Evangelii Nuntiandi* spoke about the incarnation of the Christian message with the word "inculturation," that is, the reciprocal process of enlivening the Christian message through the cultural heritage, and giving the cultural heritage its direction in the Christian message. Simply put, the document encouraged de-Europeanizing the Christian message.

United States theologians understood the importance of this inculturation, also wished to develop a more responsible theology instead of a European one, but found themselves in a different situation from many of their outspoken colleagues. These other voices from around the world possessed a stronger articulated cultural identity, more easily recognizable, with a solid historical base in symbols and life style. The United States is a society with a relatively short cultural history. Thus a strong clash with the positions of other cultures was inevitable. For example, in the United States, which is very much a Western culture and largely comprised of immigrant people from many cultures, a strong cultural substratum did not exist as it did in Latin America with the powerful cultures solidified in Aztec, Mayan, and Incan empires. Only the native Americans in the United States of America can claim an indigenous subculture, but their size relative to Latin America has been estimated at thirty to one. The other cultures of the United States were imported, with Africans, Latin American, and Asian peoples retaining a strong community identity even across great distances. But the fact remains that no long-standing, indigenous culture dominated the United States and no cultural heritage either gifts or burdens us.

The challenge is clear: even without a strong cultural heritage, the United States has a strong societal identity for which it needs to be responsible. Granted the various mixtures of cultures within the country, how does the Christian message live in this context? From the point of view of what is examined, we are really speaking of an "insocietalization" instead of "inculturation." From the point of view of our relation to the Christian message, unlike some other cultures that were evangelized, the United States for the most part had the Christian message already living in its peoples. Hence we are not talking about an "inculturation" as if the Christian message was not already believed, but a "re-culturation" which is a constant retrieval of the Christian message within the lives of the people.

The focus becomes clearer when we add the concern of inculturation: how can a Christian live in responsible discipleship in a United States context? The answer lies in understanding both the Christian message and the American situation, and fitting them together in practical action. The theological challenge inherent in this process can be called "a practical Christology."

A practical christology straddles two categories: Christology and spirituality. Rather than being two air-tight categories that do not mix with one another, they open up to one another. Spirituality is the pattern of life that one lives, formed from the values that make up the core of one's life. Spiritualities can be particular or general. University students have a spirituality, as do mothers and fathers. They also can have a more clearly identified spirituality, such as Franciscan, Jesuit, or Dominican. All live their spirituality within the American society, shaped by its values. If one chooses to judge the book in terms of these categories, on the one hand it is a Christology, and on the other hand it is a spirituality of Discipleship. These categories, however, need not box us in by their seemingly clear distinctions. Because I examine Christology with a view to what Jesus calls us to and discipleship as a response to that invitation in our United States situation, my preference is to call the entire process a practical Christology. Its method is contextual: we examine the life situation in critical relation to the Christian message as a lived discipleship.

To live discipleship in a responsible way, attentive to both the Christian message and the United States situation, requires an examination of the particular characteristics, values, drives, hopes, and messes, successes, and failures of American peoples. An exhaustive analysis would be impossible, because of its scope and because the society is always changing. Distinctive principles and values that constitute American society can be identified, however. Thus the values with which we make our society, test our laws, and found our rights as citizens, can serve to introduce many other characteristics and attitudes. The next section will identify these traits of life in the United States.

UNITED STATES CHARACTERISTICS: THE DECLARATION OF INDEPENDENCE

The story goes that an old bellman had been in the steeple since early in the morning of July 4, 1776, when the delegates gathered in Pennsylvania's brick State House. Not until the deliberations finished in the evening did the young boy stationed at the door below clap his hands and shout, "Ring! Ring!" This was the signal to all the world of the birth of a dream. Nearly fifty representatives from the colonies from New Hampshire to Georgia had pledged to this cause their lives, their fortunes, and their sacred honor. This Declaration of Independence became the spirit, symbol, and foundation of the United States of America.

This new republic formed itself upon this bedrock of the human spirit: "We hold these truths to be self-evident, that all men are created equal and that they are endowed by their Creator with certain inalienable rights, that among these are life, liberty, and the pursuit of happiness. That to secure these rights, governments are instituted among men, deriving their just powers from the consent of the governed." But rhetoric does not make a republic, or a people. The test lay in the resolve to struggle that found expression in the American Revolution. Everything could be won or lost, a country free or determined. The struggle was not one that belonged only to a single country; it belonged to the human spirit and therefore to humanity itself. The struggle was seen in terms of humanity grounded in God, led forth into a new challenge of life, liberty, and the pursuit of happiness.

This journey into the future is now over two hundred years old, a substantial but not long history by Chinese, Indian, or Egyptian standards. It is old enough, however, to constitute a tradition—and it is new because it is constantly recreating the human spirit. Freedom in its many forms is not a static right given to people on paper (although having a constitution is an important guarantee that laws will follow). One must exercise freedom in the practical choices of life. Freedom is a dynamic right, a set of choices which can be acted upon. If Jefferson, Franklin, and Washington came back to visit us today, they would be amazed at the United States, yet they would recognize its continuity. Much of what we are today was built upon and developed through the inalienable rights for which they fought.

Essentially, then, the American way of life is a dream always waiting to be realized. It is constantly being created, undone, and remade. Never will we be able to say, "We have arrived; we are finished!" We will always say "We are arriving; we have more to do."

Yet we approach the future looking in the rearview mirror of the past. Our history of decisions, growth, community, laws, mistakes, and successes stays with us. Indian reservations are a fact; slavery is a fact; detention camps for Japanese are a fact; exploitation is a fact. We live with these facts and through them. The dynamism of the past is a power we live from, or against, hoping for a creative transformation of ourselves, our society, and our world according to human rights. We commit ourselves to change within the parameters of the human person existing in society.

The basic principles by which the peoples of the United States live are set down in the Declaration of Independence. One of the extraordinary features of this document is its simplicity and compactness. Thomas Jefferson composed the document and gave it the imprint of his genius, correctly expressing the desires and dreams of the colonial representatives. It called forth great ideals and action welded together to forge a new nation. The need for concerted action has never been separated from the flesh and blood that animated what seemed an idle dream: "The Declaration of Independence contains the essential ideas of American democracy, and has remained its creed and standard through the years of its subsequent development."[1]

[1]Ralph Barton Perry, "The Declaration of Independence," *The Decla-*

One political document of approximately three thousand words contained history's most important statement toward the realization of maximum personal freedom for all members of an organized, orderly society founded on equal justice for all.[2] The Constitution contributed the due process clause, which is probably the single most effective protection of personal freedom in American law.[3]

That economic opportunity existed is without doubt. The glowing evidence of this possibility is the immigrant who, especially between 1880 and 1920 (and again today, particularly with immigration from Asia) found two new ways of living not present in the old country: personal freedom and the opportunity to convert the hard work they took for granted into economic progress.[4]

Religious opportunity existed too. People were free to live and let live, recognizing each other's differences without capitulating to them. No one religion was allowed to dominate the society. Thus was forged a new religious tolerance by which orthodoxy gave way to human rights and respect.

As stated on July 4, 1776, "Life, liberty, and the pursuit of happiness are mentioned in the great Charter; but more important than any list is the 'truth' that men possess these rights, not because of race or creed or station, but because they are human beings."[5]

The Declaration of Independence laid guidelines for the new government, but it did not determine the actual content of life, liberty, and the pursuit of happiness. True, the signers thought it was clear, as indeed it was for them. In time, however, we see that much was left vague. One drastic case in point is the issue of racism, first found in the institution of slavery, an institution partially acceptable to the founding fathers. The resolution of this conflict would involve the nation in a civil war within a century. Less bloody, but no less drastic, is the problem of sexism. Again

---

ration of Independence and the Constitution, 34th edition, ed. Earl Latham (Lexington, Mass.: D.C. Heath and Co., 1976) 9.

[2]Ira C. Corn, Jr., *The Story of the Declaration of Independence* (Los Angeles: Corwin Books, 1977) 3.

[3]Ibid., 3.

[4]Ibid., 3.

[5]Ibid., 266.

unforeseen by the founding fathers, women's liberation movements have brought a true revolution not only in rights but in ways of thinking. They have tested the authenticity and honesty of the basic rights spelled out in the Declaration of Independence.

The abiding significance of the document, however, would lie in the few sentences that begin, "We hold these truths to be self-evident."[6] There a quality of timelessness and universality entered into what might otherwise have been merely a national document. A perennial expression of human hope came alive: "Congress made these 'truths' official American doctrine by adopting them at the beginning of the history of the Republic."[7] The Declaration of Independence harks back to a philosophy of human rights, based on an appeal to reason, or the common sense of reasonable people.

Jefferson and his contemporaries believed that the rights expressed came from natural law given by God, and therefore no man could take them away. Liberty was right and God intended that all should have it, even in the face of tyrants. In our day a tyrant need not be a king, or a government; it can be media, business, drugs, or other addictions that cause us to turn over our freedom to someone or something else. More than repudiating a king (and herein lies the strength of this timeless document and its exuberant expression of human spirit) the framers of the Declaration must have sensed that they were building a republic on the cornerstone of the rights of free individuals. That republic would then try to translate into human law and social institutions the laws of the moral universe.

The United States today has not lost its identity within the moral universe. America sees itself as rooted in the most fundamental rights of humankind, and never at the expense of another's equally true and inalienable human rights. Undoubtedly the shift to a global world of information exchange has made the certainty of these moral claims more difficult to prove. But the challenge of the United States' responsibility remains. It is our heritage. To understand this responsibility before God is the theological task of this book. It is one step toward that responsibility to ourselves, our heritage, and our brothers and sisters throughout the world.

[6]Ibid., 88.
[7]Ibid., 88.

The Declaration of Independence does not provide a frame for government. That came in the Constitution. It also does not provide a pattern for human society, a specific program for the present, or a blueprint for the future. Instead it contains a body of abiding truth. The Constitution expresses our devotion to a government of laws, not men. But the Declaration serves as a perpetual reminder of the purpose of these laws, of the only valid purpose of all law: to provide a society within which all people can enjoy the largest feasible degree of liberty and attain the fullest measure of happiness. What exactly this looks like is not specified. It is the spirit of the United States.

Perhaps the most eloquent testimony of the Declaration's power over a political servant is that of Abraham Lincoln who, on his way to be inaugurated as President, on Washington's birthday in 1861, said in Independence Hall:

> I have never had a feeling politically that did not spring from the sentiments embodied in the Declaration of Independence. . . . I have often inquired of myself what great principle or idea it was that kept this Confederacy so long together. It was not the mere matter of the separation of the Colonies from the motherland; but that sentiment in the Declaration of Independence which gave liberty, not alone to the people of this country, but, I hope, to the world, for all future time. It was that which gave promise that in due time the weight would be lifted from the shoulders of all men.[8]

The words "life, liberty, and the pursuit of happiness" describe actions that take place in the concrete world. Life is not a stagnant category; it is dynamic and becoming. Liberty is not found like a deep-sea treasure chest; it is an act of decision-making that makes freedom explicit. The pursuit of happiness signifies an action, or pursuit, that is currently taking place. The content of life, liberty, and the pursuit of happiness is not given by *any* document. And limitations do exist. These restrictions will be found, among other places, in the legal system that decides cases and establishes precedents. For our purpose it is not necessary to trace the history of "life, liberty, and the pursuit of happiness." It is enough to recog-

---

[8]Ibid., 268.

nize that the content remains open-ended despite its two hundred year history.

These three characteristics mark us as United States Americans. They also indicate our drive to situate our truths in the experience of people, the *demos,* or democracy, of a people. To this extent, a deeply-rooted practical expression of who we are to one another forms us as a people. This earthiness has yielded the philosophical harvest of pragmatism in our intellectual tradition—a distinctively American philosophy.

Life, liberty, and the pursuit of happiness are interrelated. The way that I will use them with each theme is to begin with life as the most basic expression of humanity. Decisions, labeled as liberty, are possible because life exists. The pursuit of happiness expresses the ways we use our liberty and the goals we wish to pursue. Pursuing these goals brings life which issues in new freedoms, and so the cycle continues. Examined closely, the three qualities are interrelated and mutually enhance one another, so that to remove one of them does violence to our sense of completeness. Who can think in terms of life and liberty only, or life and the pursuit of happiness only?

A New York Times/CBS News poll of July 17, 1988, immediately before the 1988 presidential primaries, showed the following according to religious preference. Democrats were fifty-eight percent Protestant of which forty-one percent were white; Republicans were sixty-five percent Protestant of which sixty-two percent were white; Democrats were twenty-eight percent Catholic; Republicans were twenty-two percent Catholic; Democrats were two percent Jewish; Republicans were one percent Jewish; Democrats were five percent other and six percent none; Republicans were three percent other and seven percent none. By religious preference, Catholics fall almost equally into both parties, with slightly higher numbers in the Democratic party. Most Americans consider themselves Christian, and only a small percentage have no religious preference or identity. Thus Catholics and Christians in general cannot be isolated by party, faction, or political choice. One's religious preference is not at odds with one's political affiliation. An elasticity exists between them. The question seems to be how one wishes the values of nation to be addressed.

In reflecting on an American Christology, we see one boundary of the question circumscribed by the concept of a nation. Left alone, a nation might make decisions of benefit to itself. If other countries are introduced, however, the nation might change those decisions because they are harmful to others. Thus what we are searching for is a wider context than a nation. The nations of the earth derive from, and serve, human beings. The wider context for judging a single country's decisions must be humanity. For the Christian, humanity is understood in relation to God the Father of Jesus. Whereas we might not all agree on who God is or what God asks of us, we can all agree, for the most part, upon those things that make us human. The declaration of human rights not only for the citizens of one country but also for every human person is important and necessary. The acceptance of these basic rights by all nations is equally important and necessary. Perhaps in time we can agree upon additional rights that constitute humanity. Incrementally, by resisting negative factors that dehumanize everyone, we positively contribute to the humanization of the world.

Politics is the art of the possible. Not everyone receives everything that the common good seeks. Sometimes compromises in procedure must be made. Hopefully compromises on human rights will never be necessary.

Politics are an important dimension of a country, a nation, a people. The Christian disciple accepts this political responsibility and participates in the national conversation on what constitutes the common good, and how we are to proceed in its pursuit. Politics are not a necessary evil, not a sordid, dirty job, not an occupation that a Christian should not be involved in, as if it were antithetical to Christianity. That the political dimension can be evil does not change the reality that it is an important part of every society. In principle, politics need Christian values and discipleship in order to free others to find God and one another.

In summary, we live within the framework of the United States society under the guiding spirit of the Declaration of Independence. We can and do make history happen, because of our values and through our characteristically blended expression of those values. Though we cannot undo history, we can transform its effects as the struggle for black and women's rights indicates. The society that we live in is constantly being made, broken, and refashioned through the specific history now over two hundred years old.

We live in society and are influenced by it. We bring our own hopes, dreams, and goals into a creative relationship with others in society. We determine the content of life, liberty, and happiness through our actions.

For the Christian, discipleship is lived within this society. Christian values can oppose, support, or transform society. The characteristics of life, liberty, and the pursuit of happiness are rights with which a Christian disciple agrees. To live Christian discipleship in the United States is to live one's life for self, others, and God in loving imitation of Jesus the Christ. Thus United States discipleship is not self-serving or even other-serving, but a service to self and others grounded in God. A United States discipleship is one that serves humanity around the globe, through the responsibilities grasped through the living American culture and society.

Moreover, God speaks to us through society and culture. As history attests, God speaks in ways that we understand, ways in which we find God's presence, symbols that we understand. To accept the incarnation of Jesus as God made flesh is to accept the consequences of that act: that God deals with us through our world. Society is one way that God is made known. Yet to know God requires a discerning heart that recognizes the voice, presence, and movements of God in events. This is not always easy, yet to be a disciple means to follow Christ wherever he leads. Like the disciples on the way to Emmaus, do we recognize him in the events that happen, in the words spoken, in the burning of our own hearts?

How can we live this Christian discipleship in the United States today? What are the strengths and weaknesses of our society; what is its challenge to us as disciples? Do we know what it means to be Christian? Can we live the life to which Christ calls us? These are the questions that we will answer in the following chapters. We will take eight themes from Jesus' preaching, present their significance to the center of Jesus' message, ask how they challenge our entire Christian perspective, and show how the characteristics of American society challenge and extend our discipleship today.

Part II

The Themes of Discipleship

The purpose of this Christology is not to repeat scriptural research. That vast undertaking is the work of many scholars throughout the world, and the focus of many Christologies recently written. This Christology draws upon that significant contribution in order to move toward the pastoral application specifically in a United States context. Thus Scripture scholarship will be used to the extent that it allows good practical judgments about the meaning of the message and its implications for discipleship.

The message of Jesus is here presented in eight themes. They were neither chosen at random nor selected merely as an organizing principle. On the contrary, they are derived from the preaching of Jesus as recorded in the Scriptures, particularly the Gospels. Each theme is constitutive of the whole Christian message. To remove any one of them is to destroy the integrity of the message. Likewise, each theme requires the others.

The first theme is the kingdom of God which is the content of Jesus' preaching. Jesus did not preach about himself but the kingdom of God present in our midst. The second theme is the only command that a Christian is obliged to follow in this kingdom: love of God and love of neighbor. If one understands Christlike love then everything else falls into place. The third theme recognizes both sin and the obstacles to loving; it is the theme of conversion. We all are fallible human beings with limits and consequent sinfulness. The fourth theme is the goal of the kingdom: salvation for all. The message is sent from God to all through Jesus. Fifth is the invitation to proclaim this message in the example of service to others—the theme of mission. Sixth is the binding together of

37

broken lives, before God and one another; it is the theme of forgiveness and reconciliation. Seventh, if we accept the invitation to
follow Jesus, then we enter into discipleship. Finally, disciples share
a common discipleship through the guidance of one Holy Spirit.
This is what we call Church and this is our eighth theme.

Scripture scholars and theologians agree on the centrality of these
themes to the Christian message. Other themes, of course, extend
the meaning of these eight into the practicality of living discipleship. Compassion, concern for the poor, social justice, prayer, humility, and perseverance are some of the other themes implied. Thus
the eight are not exhaustive, but they do gather up the others and
point to the centrality of Jesus' message.

The purpose of identifying these themes is to show the areas
which are the specific responsibilities of the United States. Our
responsibilities are to the Christian message, American society, and
global humanity. Both the Christian message and global humanity find their point of entry into people's lives through the society
in which we live. Our discipleship will necessarily reflect these
characteristics and their interaction.

Each treatment of the eight themes has five parts. It begins with
scriptural support for the particular theme, thus the Gospels of Matthew, Mark, Luke, and John will figure prominently. This material is gathered from Scripture scholars and, although not
complete—many books have been written on biblical Christology—
represent the results of biblical scholarship.

Secondly, the scriptural support will be used within a systematized explanation of the meaning of these themes. For this I have
used a set of three relationships between God, Jesus, and us, to
which I have given the simple name of a triad.

Thirdly, a retrieval of the tradition for further explanations,
dimensions, additions, and insights will be done. This third step
allows the scriptural and systematic material to be brought forward
together, and thus helps us critically correlate the Christian message with our time and place.

Fourth, each theme will be fitted into the United States situation from the perspective of American characteristics. The con-
clusions suggest acceptance of some societal values and the rejection
of others. Because many possible courses of action can be taken,
the suggestions are a fluid model for living discipleship.

Fifth, to move each reader from a general model to an awareness of their personal responsibility, I have included a set of questions for reflection. Ideally they are not meant to stop at personal reflection, but to continue in conversation with others. This final step would best be taken in a study group, classroom, parish program, or some other communal form.

In summation, each chapter will begin with the meaning of the particular theme, move to systematic understanding in the form of its relationship to God, Jesus, and us (a triad), explain whatever retrieval of this tradition for today entails, and clarify the challenge that the theme presents us in the context of the United States through the characteristics of life, liberty, and the pursuit of happiness. Each chapter ends with a set of questions aimed to articulate one's personal responsibility and its implications for all people.

Theme 1

THE KINGDOM OF GOD:
THE PLAN AND ITS INVITATION

Without Jesus there would be no Christianity. The earliest Christian disciples were eyewitnesses to his words, deeds, death and resurrection. But Jesus did not care about his own importance; he was a person with a message not of his own but of God, whom he addressed as *abba* or "dad." That message was spoken in words and lived in deeds, and the integrity of what Jesus said and did was judged by others. Thus his message and mission join together.

Our question becomes, "What did Jesus preach?" In one sense his message was his whole life or what we call the "Jesus Event." But we must also ask whether Jesus spoke more directly about the meaning of his life. The answer from Scripture is that he did. The Gospels call this message "the kingdom of God." Thus, in his words, Jesus told us how to understand and interpret the significance of his actions, even to his death on the cross.

When some university students were asked to explain what the kingdom of God meant today, they gave various definitions: "the perfect place which Christians strive for," "a place after death," "heaven," "an abstract existence with God," "the final and ultimate resting place after death," "the Church," "the realm of timeless knowledge and freedom," and "salvation."

On the instinctive level these responses correctly present the kingdom as a realm related to God; and on the conceptual level they indicate the difficulty of defining the concept's relevance for our culture. Its "timeless," "abstract," and "heavenly" dimension characterize Jesus' preaching as having little relevance to our earthly world—a position diametrically opposed to that taken by the Gospels. The richness and dynamism within this concept of the kingdom needs to be retrieved for our discipleship today.

But, because of our history, explaining this central concept is not an easy task. Americans labor beneath romantic concepts and ambivalent emotions about kings and kingdoms that were not part of Jesus' understanding. To begin with the earliest history of the United States, Americans fought a revolution in order to free themselves from the rule of a king. Then we made a declaration of our independence and forged new democratic principles into a constitution of, by, and for the people. Ours was a democratic society built on principles that came about in direct opposition to the arbitrary power and wealth of kings; a democracy based upon individual rights that could not be violated, where everyone was "king" and no one was, where power was handed over to the people by social contract. To return to the rule of a king by choice is now unthinkable. In a true sense, our nation was birthed in direct opposition to a king and kingdom. Deep in our collective emotion is the feeling that kingdoms are historically archaic and tyrannical, determining a person's worth by service to the king.

Moreover, what we know of kingdoms derives not from our immediate political experience but from our literary knowledge of stories that begin "Once upon a time," or ancient legends of King Arthur and his Knights of the Round Table, or wicked queens and a beautiful Fairy Princess. We also know of kings and queens who still reign throughout the world, such as Queen Elizabeth II of England. Although kings and kingdoms are concepts we readily comprehend, we never consider them as a real political choice for ourselves. Rather, we see them as remnants of the past to which we choose never to return.

Because the kingdom of God is so central to our tradition, we need to retrieve that past and bring it forward to our present situation so that we may first understand it before we decide how to live in it as disciples.

The Kingdom of God in Scripture

Our first theme is the kingdom of God. We want to know how this relates to the Jesus Event. To do so we will examine its importance in the Gospels, at times including other scriptural references in order to understand what particular passages would have meant in the time of Jesus. Our attempt is to bring that first century's understanding from its semitic and hellenistic context into the context of America in the twentieth century. The purpose is not to make the original context American—that would be impossible— but to let the freshness and challenge of the Jesus Event break like a spiritual wave upon us anew.

When Jesus emerged from his baptism, after receiving his identity and mission from the Father, the first words that he preached were: "The time is fulfilled, and the kingdom of God is at hand; repent, and believe in the gospel" (Mark 1:15; Matt 4:17). The Gospels tell us that Jesus' central proclamation was the coming of the kingdom of God. It is the theme of the parables, the reason for the miracles. In Matthew, John the Baptizer's function and purpose is to announce the coming of the kingdom. Jesus did not preach about himself, nor did he make the recognition of his divinity a condition of belief. Quite clearly, he preached that the kingdom of God was present, breaking into the world, through his person, work, and words. The dominant image by which we understand Jesus' preaching is the kingdom of God.

The responses of students to the phrase "the kingdom of God" start where Jesus probably did, with the current understanding of kingdom. Then Jesus turned that concept into an expression of God's reign. Kingdom does not define God's relationship with us so much as extend that relationship to everyone and everything, thereby describing the reign where God holds sway.

No more important concept expresses Christian spiritual life than the kingdom of God. When Jesus sent out the seventy-two disciples, they were to preach that the kingdom of God was at hand. When the disciples asked Jesus to teach them how to pray, he told them to address God familiarly, as a child calls his or her father "dad" *(abba)*. Then Jesus said to ask for those favors that are important. The first petition that we make, after holding God holy ("Our Father who art in heaven, hallowed be thy name"), is to pray for the coming of the kingdom ("Thy kingdom come, thy will be done"). This praying for the coming of the kingdom, the process of its inbreaking now in this world, is the heart of how Jesus taught us to pray. The kingdom is central to discipleship.

Let us examine the term itself. "Kingdom of God" and "kingdom of heaven" are synonymous, with the term "kingdom of heaven" confined to Matthew who, probably because of the Jewish-Christian respect for God's name, substituted "heaven" for "God." The term is used frequently: Mark uses it thirteen times, Matthew twenty-five, Luke six, and John uses it twice. The word "kingdom" in Greek is *basileia,* which is translated as "reign." The idea is not limited to a piece of land or territory with walls and fences governed by a king, but expresses the rule (power, sway, influence) of God as activated and working its way through the world.

The image of kingdom relies upon spatial and temporal images which in themselves are never sufficient. Because this kingdom is synonymous with where God is, both in heaven and on earth, it cannot be identical with a space or a territory. Nevertheless we know that God's kingdom will take shape in this world. The kingdom will not be identifiable with any of the world's forms; however, it will be neither a government nor a church. These serve the kingdom. Likewise, the kingdom of God cannot be identical with a time, past, present, or future. It came definitively in the person of Jesus, exists now in the ever-changing present, and always points forward to the future. We call this always-future looking dimension eschatological (end time). One of Jesus's earliest titles was "the eschatological prophet." Thus the kingdom possesses a two-fold dimension of "already here" and "not yet completed." Jesus ushered in the kingdom, it exists now in our present, and it looks toward its completion in the future when all is brought under its reign. Thus the disciple can never sit back in comfort and say, "Now it is finished." Rather, we declare at all times, "It is happening!"

The totality of the kingdom is not grasped by any particular culture, society, civilization, or people. Every age stands under its judgment and strives to realize this kingdom as best it can. Although we participate in the building up of the kingdom, it remains always a gift of God and is God's very presence with us. As Jesus showed us, the kingdom manifests itself in words and deeds, events, and signs. Its effect is to unite us in a love relationship that tradition has understood as a covenant, or pact, or contract, initiated by God to us. God does not remain apart from us but breaks the silence and closes the distance between the divine and the human.

Then God awaits our response. A covenant always carries the sense of a startling invitation which transcends us; a holy, unfathomable mystery that surrounds us, lures us, and grasps us. We either accept or reject this invitation. Not choosing to accept the invitation is a stalling tactic that also amounts to a disguised form of rejection. The marvel of God is the invitation to *participate* in bringing about the kingdom. By performing acts of love, justice, and peace we allow God's kingdom to be present, we act cooperatively with God to transform the world, and we become ambassadors to our neighbors, urging them to become participants in this kingdom.

"King" is an important concept throughout Judaic history and, no doubt, influenced Jesus' own understanding as well as that of the people to whom he spoke. Whereas the idea of a king was one of the most important concepts in the Old Testament, the use of the phrase "kingdom of God" does not appear, although "kingdom" is used in relation to God about twelve times.[1]

Monarchies in the Far East at the time of the Old Testament were of three types. The first comprised the petty kings of the Palestinian cities, often foreigners, who ruled with the support of the military. The second group, represented by Egyptian and Mesopotamian kings, were considered divinely ordained and held political power for the good of the empire. The third group, ethnically related to the Hebrews, had their roots in the military leadership of the native armies.

In Judaic history, the term "king" usually designates a male sovereign who exercised power over an independent nation and had the right to transmit the royal power to his descendants. Kings assumed three roles: the military leader of the nation, the supreme judge, and, in the earliest period at least, an officiating priest. The covenant with Yahweh, according to some scholars, was a royal covenant. Therefore, an earthly king was thought by some to be an act of apostasy, a repudiation of the forsworn covenant with God. As learned in the Exodus event, Yahweh was a king like no other. By the time of Saul and David, monarchical structure was allowed by God who anointed them kings. But no one missed the clear reality that these kings served Yahweh alone, and that God

[1]For information on king and kingdom, see *The Interpreter's Dictionary of the Bible,* New York: Abingdon Press, 1962) 3:11–14.

brought his kingdom to earth in the peace and prosperity these kingdoms represented. Even when the monarchy of Israel began, these kings (for example: Saul, David, Solomon) were considered vassals of Yahweh. Through anointing, the king of Israel became sacrosanct. David did not dare kill Saul. An intimacy between God and the king existed, and bestowed blessings upon the people. But unlike other contemporary monarchs, the pharaohs of Egypt and the Caesars in Rome, the king of Israel never attained the status of deity.

To many people, the hereditary lineage of the king (from David to Solomon) violated God's freedom to choose the king. For this and other reasons, the ten tribes to the north split off and were later conquered by the Assyrians. Throughout Judaic history to the time of Jesus, the kingdom represented by David, historically romanticized, remained a symbol of peace and prosperity, justice and security. It became an eschatological symbol of what could be, in the face of what was. When Jesus spoke of a king, he entered into the symbolic expectations of people influenced by these thoughts. Yet, quite extraordinarily, he presented his listeners with the unique concept of a king who serves us! The understanding of the kingdom became a reign over the human heart and its actions in the world.

In the Synoptic Gospels the term "kingdom of God" designates the central theme of Jesus' preaching and mission. Its use seems to come from Jesus himself. Its meaning goes beyond any other usage at the time. In most cases the "kingdom" belongs to God but in a few passages it belongs to "the Son of Man" (Matt 13:41, 16:28) or to Jesus himself (Matt 20:21, Luke 1:33; 22:29-30; 23:42). The connection to the "Son of Man" is an important one.

The "Son of Man" is a complex title used in the Gospels both as a reference to Jesus as an ordinary person who is a servant (Ezek 2), and with reference to the apocalyptic book of Daniel (7:9 ff.) where the identity of the Son of Man is revealed in the following dream. While the heavenly court is convened, "one like the Son of Man" (that is, an ordinary person) comes on the clouds and is presented to the "Ancient One" (that is, God) from whom he receives dominion, glory, and kingship. Nations and peoples of every language and race serve this Son of Man whose kingship will not be destroyed. The kingdom brought by Jesus is truly that of God's dominion, glory, and kingship to all people everywhere and at all times, as Daniel describes.

The kingdom of God arrives in the present moment. In the person of Jesus, the kingdom becomes imminent, "at hand," breaking forth even as he speaks and acts. The power of God is manifest now, in this world, at this time. We learn that God is a God of action, compassion, care, and immediacy—a God who does not get tied up in red tape or bureaucracy. The present moment belongs to God. Both the words and deeds of Jesus, his parables and miracles, demonstrate God's victorious presence as always present. They show God's power operating in this world with the promise of a new age whose morning has already dawned, and whose day is yet to be finished.

The kingdom is to be consummated in the future. Jesus tells us that only God knows the time and place of this consummation. Our task is to live within this horizon of faith and to act in complete trust of God. The point is clear: we are to be vigilant and industrious for the kingdom until it arrives. In the meantime, the kingdom is growing to completion like a mustard seed, silently and imperceptibly.

In the Gospels, Jesus' mission becomes understood within the context of the kingdom. Each Gospel begins Jesus' mission at baptism and moves forward to Jesus' final surrender at his death on the cross. Even the infancy narratives of Matthew and Luke point to Jesus' mission at baptism. His life and death are an undivided unity. His life interprets his death, and his death interprets his life. The mystery of salvation is in his person and is sealed forever and definitively in the coming kingdom of God. The inauguration of God's definitive reign in Jesus and the continual process of redemption find their foundation in the death and resurrection of Jesus. The death-resurrection is hyphenated to indicate the indissoluble unity of this act and its related dynamism from which Christianity takes its life. The Christian disciple turns love loose in the salvific manner of this life-death-resurrection, which we call the Jesus Event.

This kingdom resides not in a heavenly world apart from us but where sin does its damage—in this world. Just as sin subverts this world by the powers of evil, so must salvation occur here, not in an already saved heaven. The kingdom includes what we mean by heaven but it begins by radically overturning the power of Satan in this world and aligning us to God. Those who stand against the power of Satan are gathered into God's community, which will be an instrumental life force in the exercise of God's rule. It will be a sign, a leaven, a light of hope for the present generation and a sign of the future consummation when God's reign is complete.

In this interim time, evil will not go away. Life remains a battle with evil from which the disciple is not exempt. A most sobering statement about how the kingdom of Satan will be dealt with is Matthew's parable of the wheat and weeds (Matt 13:24-30). The sower planted his wheat by day and his enemy came at night to sow weeds. As the plants grew up, the workers found the weeds growing together with the wheat. They went to their master. The master told them to let both co-exist for now, but at harvest time reap them together and then separate the wheat from the weeds. The weeds would be burned. Thus the Christian disciple cannot expect evil to disappear in this world. As long as we have free will to love God, we possess the capacity not to love. Only God will bring evil to extinction, when all is in God.

Matthew goes a step further and says that the kingdom of Satan resides both outside the Church and, unfortunately, inside the Church. He indicates where: in false speech, failures in loving, lukewarmness toward discipleship, failure to forgive, and false prophets. The devil will try to use people in many ways to change them. Just as Peter is called "Satan" by Jesus when he tries to tell Jesus that he need not suffer and die as Messiah, so too will Satan tempt others to deviate from a discipleship obedient to God. No disciples in any place, time, structure, or relationship can relax their efforts to resist evil.

Although its completion is in the future, the reign of God has already broken into the world and it is "good news" (gospel) for all. The process of salvation has entered a new age *(eschaton)*. Cosmic in scope and synonymous with doing God's will, it cannot be evaded. Rather than dividing the present and future, the kingdom brings together the present and future in an organic unity. Though not identical to the past, the future emerges out of the past and builds upon the present moment of love, like two people who say "I do" at their marriage ceremony and live this fidelity out in the future. Whether we see the future breaking into the present or the present breaking into the future, a continuity exists between the two dimensions, and it opens the possibility of greater human involvement with God.

The kingdom comes in word and deed. Our reliance upon God's loving presence requires us to become like little children who trust God's loving involvement with us. We believe that it is God who starts our existence, sustains it, and is the finish of it. This reign of God imposes the same divine qualities towards others: love, forgiveness, and service. It is open to all comers, especially those who have little to recommend them; it welcomes the poor and the lowly and those who suffer for righteousness (Matt 5:3, 10; 19:14; Mark 10:14; Luke 6:20; 18:16). For God, to be human is all that is necessary to be invited to the kingdom; yet to remain in the kingdom requires vigilance and perseverance. For those who wish to enter, a change of heart is required, symbolized in the word "repentance." One must turn to and with God (that is, be converted), which requires one to lean on God with all one's weight (faith). One who lives trusting God in word and deed enters the kingdom. To be and live in God is our salvation.

In John's Gospel, an important change begins to take place. "Kingdom of God" is replaced by "life." This gradual change in the use of kingdom, at least in John's tradition, signals (1) perhaps a preference for the meaning that "life" gives to kingdom and (2) the stronger personal bond between the believer, Jesus, the Father, and the Spirit. Life results: not human life or life from below, but divine life from above. God gifts us with a new and real love that is life, and with a life that is love. We are swept into the life of God, which is a love story, and we are empowered by that life.

The Triad: God-Jesus-Us

Jesus puts us into a three-fold set of relationships: God and Jesus, Jesus and us, God and us. By looking at these relationships from every side, we gain a new perspective on the Jesus Event, and a better understanding of the various commitments implied. Our method employed here is called contextual-relational. Contextual means it begins in the Jesus Event; relational means it examines the various obligations and commitments involved. We will refer to this method in its three-fold concern: the triad.

If we begin from the perspective of God's relation to us, the kingdom is God's desire. It provides on the one hand our goal, destiny, and fulfillment, and on the other hand sums up our relation with God. Under a king, the person is defined by his or her service to the king. To our astonishment, this king serves us! The normal understanding of people serving the king becomes inverted; those who serve become those who are served. The last become first, the adult becomes like the little child, the master becomes servant, the poor become rich. We become God's purpose for the kingdom.

We are dependent upon God, communicated with by God, and participants in the reality which God wishes for us. God desires our happiness even more than we do. The kingdom of God symbolizes that God commands all cosmic forces, that divine power and love operate victoriously, and that fulfillment is here. At the same time this majestic and sovereign God of glory and power does not remain apart from us in a transcendent realm of heaven. God is present in people and places that seemingly cannot manifest God, even places of powerlessness and degradation. In the Beatitudes we learn that God is in the poor, the naked, the starving, the thirsty. This sovereign God is also the humble God. God's victory can become present even in apparent defeat. No person, place, or thing escapes God's presence and love. To cooperate with that power and accept that love, however, remains our free choice.

Next, we will take the perspective of Jesus. The kingdom of God and its content are revealed through Jesus. With the intimate knowledge of a son who knows the secrets of his father's heart, Jesus preaches the kingdom, makes it present, and shows us that it is proceeding, yet it is incomplete. He invites others into the kingdom's power and reign through their free commitment to love as God loves. Love centers the call but it includes many other ways of responding, in and through our relation to our personal, social, and historical development. Jesus lived and died with the kingdom as his message and gift. We come into the kingdom through Jesus; he is the way to the Father. We find in Jesus our example, our lord, our savior, God with us, the Word of God made flesh, the Son of God who makes us his brothers and sisters under the same father, who is supremely human and divine at the same time, and who invites us to follow him in discipleship.

When Jesus called people to faith, they entered into the reign of the kingdom, that is, they entered under its power, rule, or sway. Brought under the reign of God, one acts according to the demands of the kingdom which can be summed up in one command: love God and neighbor. Christian discipleship is really quite simple and uncomplicated. Once connected to the kingdom through faith, the disciple acts in Christlike love.

We find that God is committed in and to those acts of love. God is present, dynamic, gracious, and better known through each free choice to love. God authenticates those choices in the peace, joy, happiness, and integrity that result. Every disciple discovers this divine presence in her or his life. The future is open ended for our participation and creativity in loving. While the kingdom does not tell us precisely what form our action will take in the practical order, it never relents in informing us that every action must be a loving one and that God's fidelity is committed there. The Christian, therefore, enjoys remarkable freedom to act in concert with God in bringing the kingdom about: in self, in personal relationships, in society, and in the world.

Finally, from the perspective of ourselves, the kingdom has entered human living. Salvation overtakes sin in our history. We are not slaves but friends who take responsibility given to us by God through Jesus to help bring about this kingdom on earth. We extend the works and words of Jesus in our own lives, by our own actions, and by the grace of God. The actions and words of Jesus remain a constant source of our own sanctification. Sanctification means finding our actions a source of continued, deepened unleashing of God's power and presence within us.

In our struggle to believe, the question of whether God exists is not the dilemma. For a disciple, the question is, how much can I trust God? Just when we think we have given everything to God, God asks for more. Each day, each life, each death seems to ask of us more and more trust in God. The spirituality of the disciple seems not to be one of great invincible faith, but, perhaps like Peter's, a humbler, breakable faith. The disciple is faced with the question not, "Is my faith strong enough now?" but "Is my faith weak enough now to let God more into my life?" Thus we come to a humbler acknowledgement that God is all in our life and that we must lean on God more and more.

The kingdom of God expresses God's relation to Jesus and the Christian disciple, and the disciple's relation to Jesus and God, and Jesus' relation to God and the disciple. No part of the relationship can be broken. Each involves and envelops the other; each requires continuing participation; each contributes to the reality of the kingdom.

Retrieving the Kingdom for Today

The concept of kingship is not a universal one. For example, "king" is not a term used in Native American cultures. Only the Nachez tribe in the Louisiana area use the word "king," perhaps because of a connection with the Aztecs.

A monarchy is, then, a type of government not known to Native Americans. In these cultures, the chief is in charge but he rules through egalitarian participation by members of the tribe. For example, in praying the Our Father, converts to Christianity from the Arapaho and Ojibwa, a Chippewa group, translate "kingdom" as "where you are" or "where you are in charge." The word designates a space God fills. It is the place of God's work or business. In many ways, this translation emphasizes the reign or power of God as it takes place here. This translation is absolutely devoid of our Western understanding of kings and kingdoms.

At the same time, heaven is a strong and rich concept among Native Americans, as is its correlative term earth. Generally accepted among all Native American tribes is a belief in an afterlife. They possess an eschatology which combines the presence of God in heaven and on earth with a future life with God. For the present, the body is buried in the earth.

Within our own ecclesial tradition, the concept of a kingdom has been downplayed in favor of other images. Perhaps the greatest example is the work of St. Augustine. In the beginning of the fifth century, he wrote a classic book explaining God's reign or power in the history of the world and called it *The City of God*. Augustine used the image of the New Jerusalem descending to earth at the end of the *Book of Revelation*. In the Roman Empire of his time, with the city of Rome being sacked and the eventual dissolution of the empire, Augustine saw a new city emerging, a city of God where a new rule took hold.

Any designation of a rule is problematic, especially in our day of competing political systems and hostility towards others. Can you imagine the problems we would have if Jesus had compared God's rule to a socialist state, a republic, an empire, a democracy, a trans-national corporation? Although the concept of kingdom and a king are historically distant from our experience, that distance might be advantageous for our emotions. The idea of a king and kingdom is dear to the Old Testament because it connotes freedom, peace, prosperity, security, and justice. God as king has the power to bring these treasured human hopes to completion. Yet the concept of the kingdom as presented by Jesus really focuses upon the human response to God's invitation, or the world of salvation as it should be lived. Jesus never calls God "king" directly, but certainly the title is implicit in every instance. Jesus also never preaches about himself, but always about the kingdom of God. If we know in our hearts peace, security, justice, prosperity, and freedom, then we know the dimensions and content of this concept of kingdom for today.

What, then, is the reality of the kingdom that we need to understand? That "kingdom" is a relational term rather than a place. It indicates the relationships that are demanded for human wholeness and holiness. The relationship is not to a world to come, as if Christians are storing up a bank account of merit in heaven, but to each other today. The parable of the last judgment asks if the hungry were fed, the naked clothed, the thirsty given to drink, and so on. What is done in *this* life becomes important. If sin occurs in this world, then the kingdom must come in this world. Heaven may be free of sin, but this world is not. God's grace is needed, and in abundance.

Historical arguments such as that of Karl Marx, who said that religion was the opium of the people, imagined existence as a kind of two layered cake: earth on one level and heaven on the other. The relationship with God, however, either enters in this world, in this society, in this culture, in this context, in this person—or it does not enter at all. God works in and through this world, which is the only one we know. Our responsibility is to preach and live the kingdom to which Jesus invited us. In a word, it is the meaning of the incarnation itself: God becomes flesh in this world for our salvation.

God is committed to the building of this kingdom and it will be present when justice and peace occur. God will be present even in the dark side of this struggle. The task of bringing the kingdom is extended to human persons: we cooperate with God's love for us when we do the works of the kingdom.

God's commitment is irrevocably made in Jesus, through a covenant that God will not take back. God has committed himself to this kingdom and to those who accept this task. The promise includes personal grace as well as social grace. A disciple's life will be full, authentic, genuine, and as fully human as possible, not in quantity but quality. A society's life will be just, peaceful, honest, and fair, and will support fully human, meaningful life.

The Church is a sign, and further, a sacrament (a symbol that does what it signifies) of God's presence in the world. Yet God works far beyond the confines of the Church. The kingdom reaches beyond the signs themselves. Whatever signs we have that show forth the kingdom in an imperfect way give us a clearer focus, a moment of luminous clarity in which we can say, "Yes, there is God's kingdom being realized." When mercy tempers justice, love leads to reconciliation, and self-renunciation overrides selfishness, then the kingdom of God is being realized. The form it takes is not as clear, for there is more than one right answer. A plurality of responses and the forms they take is possible. "To love another person" does not tell me the exact form that love will take. Two people might express their love in the commitment of marriage; when one is married or committed to religious life then the form of love respects that commitment. The variety and forms of love are true calls to love in a Christlike way. While the forms are many, the spirit of love remains one.

A caveat is needed. Too often in Christian tradition the concept of kingdom has meant an other-worldly reality, namely heaven. That God would become involved in changing the structures of this world, that true peace and justice could prevail, has seemed beyond realization. Perhaps a tinge of hopelessness about this world and its sinfulness has pervaded and destroyed any realization of the kingdom here on earth. It is always easier to see the grass greener on the other side, to find green pastures in heaven but not on earth. Humans have preferred to find the realization of the kingdom in heaven, because the redressing of wrongs and the balancing of this world's debts were too great and historically impossible to accomplish. There remains truth in this. But to over-emphasize the redressing of wrongs in heaven is not authentic to the Scriptures. The place of salvation is here on earth. A growing social awareness has been taking place in Christian consciousness, especially Catholic consciousness, about the equally important reality of the kingdom realized here and now.

To enter this kingdom, one must have faith. Faith, as we have said, means to lean on someone with all one's weight. One leans upon what is solid, and truth is the rock of faith. Faith, the Gospels tell us, comes from an act of conversion. To repent, renounce one's self, acknowledge one's dependence upon God, admit sinfulness, all are various ways of describing the motivation to become converted. One falls in love with someone greater than themself; they are awed by a goodness not their own; they stand before a fascinating mystery that envelops all that they are, and they place themself within its sphere of influence to accept its invitation. Therefore, the kingdom of God is not a recognizable form but a recognizable *relationship,* marked by Christlike qualities of love, compassion, forgiveness, and service, both personal and social.

The life of God is like the air we breathe: it gives life and sustains life. To speak about the very life of God within people is conveyed by the image of God's holy breath or spirit. Luke's Gospel most develops the understanding of the persona of the Holy Spirit. The disciple in the kingdom possesses God's very spirit, the Holy Spirit, which animates, enlivens, breathes holy life into all that the disciple is and does. As Jesus possessed God's spirit, so too the disciple finds God's presence in acts of love, compassion, and forgiveness. God's spirit breaks forth into life when we perform the acts of the kingdom of God whose fidelity abides with us. The gifts of peace and joy are two signs of the Holy Spirit that accompany our actions when they are united with God.

One might think that belonging to the kingdom brings automatic happiness. Matthew's Gospel is very enlightening here and it reflects the experience of the early communities. The kingdom of God is here, victorious, and will triumph finally at the end. In the meantime, in this interim time that we live in, the opposing kingdom of Satan will try to conquer. Doomed to failure, it can lead people astray. Until the end of time, these two opposing kingdoms will butt heads. Evil is not done away with, but it is never triumphant: love is. Therefore the disciple will face evil in his or her life and be tested by it. "Do not put us to the test," we daily pray from the Our Father, "but deliver us from evil." No disciple can be lax, lukewarm, or lack vigilance. As Jesus was tempted, so will we be. As Jesus was mistreated, so will we be. As Jesus was crucified, so must we be ready to do the same. We must pick up our cross and follow him.

Life, Liberty, and the Pursuit of Happiness

We now will examine the theme of Christ within the characteristics of the United States. We begin with the basic gift called life, its possible decisions (liberty) and its goals (the pursuit of happiness). The three characteristics are intertwined and enhance one another.

The understanding of the kingdom of God remains to be put into practice in our day. Certainly the kingdom extends beyond any attempt to completely define it. The best that we can do is to begin exploring its dimensions in the United States of America. Perhaps some have never thought how pervasive this message of Jesus is in our lives. Perhaps others have never seen the all-inclusiveness of the kingdom through our personal, social, cultural, and societal responsibilities. In this section we will seek to make the kingdom specific and applicable to our lives. The section is not meant to be exhaustive but only suggestive of ways of following Jesus. We can call these reflections a United States spirituality of discipleship.

In order to specify the United States context, we will use the three constitutive American traits from our Declaration of Independence: life, liberty, and the pursuit of happiness. I am fully aware that these three do not account for all American traits. Drawing that kind of comprehensive picture would be a herculean task. My contention here is that these three characteristics remain at the core of American life. As indicated in the previous chapter, we will begin with life as the basis for liberty which, in turn, gives us the possibility of pursuing happiness. Happiness brings new life which brings new dimensions of liberty and the pursuit of happiness. The exercise of these inalienable rights also constitutes the most distinctive responsibilities of an American discipleship.

LIFE

The kingdom of God is a political image. It expresses the gathering up of people into a social unity under the power and sway of God. This kingdom is not to be equated with the Christendom of Constantine in the fourth century, Charlemagne in the nineth century, democracy in the eighteenth century, or Vatican City in the nineteenth century. The kingdom of God cuts across all governments because it is not bound by land frontiers or social contracts. This kingdom belongs to the heart of human beings and is the truth of human life. The political and societal image is an analogy, similarity-in-difference. Yes, God's kingdom gathers us all in love; no, it is not identical with any political and societal structure, value, or ideology, yet it judges and includes all political and societal structures, values, and ideologies. The disciple recognizes that just as life is lived in a society and influences that society, so does a person's faith give value to a person's life and necessarily impact that society. The disciple accepts responsibility for the society and asks it to support the values of true human life.

A democracy such as ours finds its values in the people. Christian disciples call upon the people to find the truth of democratic values in Jesus. In our political and societal affairs, love in its many forms makes the best policy and establishes the best ways of proceeding. Why? Because these values are the ones which allow us to be human. The life that we share depends upon our legislative, executive, and judicial values. The way we call upon one another is part and parcel of the values that we hold and desire. Hence, disciples cannot abrogate their responsibilities when it comes to political and societal policies, laws, and administration.

Voting is one way of entering into this responsibility, but not just any kind of voting. Disciples need greater awareness of the issues and values involved. This might mean needing more information. Discipleship might imply, for some, becoming resource people who can acquire and give the information required, making it available for those who cannot research it but wish to be informed of the data. Or, it might imply asking others for the information. The point is that voting is an opportunity to exercise one's Christian discipleship, it is not merely a "political" act.

LIBERTY

The kingdom of God frees individuals to be their best selves. It is up to Christian individuals to cooperate with God's work within, around, and ahead of themselves. Nevertheless, society is filled with people who are not free. Oftentimes they are trapped in grinding poverty, economic deprivation, unemployment, drugs, paralyzing fear, insecurity, or spiralling violence. Destructive tendencies exist both in individuals and in societal interaction. Without the intention of doing so, society can and does oppress, dehumanize, and victimize persons. The poor get poorer, the needy go unaided, medical help is not forthcoming, and the lure of the good life traps others who either become desperate or turn to violence and crime. One could view these various relationships in terms of power. The power of God to make us free fights with the power of destruction which enslaves us.

While many uses of freedom are possible for the disciple, it might be more helpful to focus on abuses of freedom. We shall draw a line, beyond which we will not go. "Here we will stand for the sake of all people" we say; this is the bottom line. A disciple may not say, "It is someone else's problem." It is the Christian's problem. When elderly women are robbed and raped, when children are abused, when people wander the street in search of food and shelter, these are the disciples' problems. Exactly what is to be done is never clear; that something can be done is sure. While disciples can do something within their personal lives, they must also work on the causes of evil in the society and call themselves to implement Christian values in society. Agencies, taxation allotments, use of revenues by government ideally should reflect the concerns of the society. Human needs cannot be overlooked. Can one make some time, use a talent for a while, give support in these areas? What can the disciple do?

PURSUIT OF HAPPINESS

The kingdom of God tells us that Christlike love in its many dimensions is true happiness. In the United States we can often narrow the pursuit of happiness to individualism. Yet the image of a kingdom and the reality it conveys is that of a social unit. Christian discipleship is not to be lived at the expense of others or for itself alone. Its invitation is always outward moving, including others, nourishing and serving others so that they too can pursue authentic happiness. "Authentic" is a word preferred to "true" because not everyone grasps the truth of the Christian faith, yet all are called to live responsibly for themselves and others. By its nature, the call of the kingdom is a social reality that shows forth love, justice, peace, and happiness. Others may come to see the truth of this way of love. Hence discipleship is always two-pronged, pointing to the individual and simultaneously to its extension into the life of society.

Disciples can work with values that are Christlike as they occur in society. Honesty, compassion, care, and generosity are only a few. Supporting environmental issues, easing hunger, supporting charities of all kinds, and promoting peace in the world are good causes. They do not have to be run by Catholics or Christians. The values are Christlike, and we can work shoulder to shoulder to see that these values come about in human life. As Vatican II stated, disciples promote Christlike values in society even when the source is other than Christian. Disciples also act against dehumanizing values, no matter what their source. The Church exists in the modern world and its relationships with this modern world are complex. Yet its message remains a consistently simple one: to live in Christlike love.

There is a challenging saying which goes, "If you were arrested for being a Christian, would there be enough evidence to convict you?" In our Church assemblies and in our society, disciples are called to be people of love. Would we be convicted as Christians by the evidence of our lives? The question is worth pondering.

The kingdom of God is a political image that signals the responsibility of the disciple to work to bring about God's reign. Disciples exercise their responsibilities by becoming active in the political and social arenas. Disciples place love at the center of their values. Practical analysis of voting issues is one way of being a disciple. Disciples must resist all attempts to dehumanize others through society's policies. Moreover, the disciple cannot retreat into individualism but must work for social values which benefit others. If individual pursuits of happiness clash, the disciple promotes those values which show love for others and resists those values which work against Christlike love.

Further Considerations

1. Personally: Where do I experience the kingdom of God in my life? What people are the exemplars of people in the kingdom?

2. United States context: What events in this country are possible signs of God's kingdom? Which events are NOT signs of the kingdom?

3. Global context: What events around the world indicate the possible presence of the kingdom of God? Which do not?

4. Church context: How does the Church show forth God's kingdom? Which aspects of the Church do not show it forth?

LOVE OF GOD AND LOVE OF NEIGHBOR: THE WAY WE LIVE

Love is one of the most commonly used words in American culture. It is applied to a variety of expressions and meanings: "I love Chinese food;" "I love that music;" "I love that dress;" "I love baseball." Bumper stickers tell us that people "love New York" or Los Angeles or some other city. People fall in love, love friends, and marry for love. Love covers a whole range of weak and strong attractions, from liking things to loving another person intimately for life.

The gospel is a story of love. This love is not a weak attraction. God's love for us begins before the gospel starts, namely in creation and in a covenant relationship from Sinai. God's outpouring of love reaches its greatest expression in the person of Jesus. That same Christlike love takes expression in each one of our lives. The return of that love as it transforms human life is discipleship. Thus, what is begun in creation is intensified in Jesus and completed in us as members of humanity.

Jesus calls us to a specific type of love: to love God above all, and to love our neighbor as ourselves. The love of God and that of neighbor are inseparable; the disciple cannot love one without the other. The reason is that love always involves a relationship. In this case, God has loved us and our neighbor, thus to love God implies loving those whom God loves. To deny love to them is to deny God himself. Because God has chosen to love others, our love for God relates us to others in such a way that the same, consistent, and integral love we give to God must also be given to others. As John the evangelist expresses it, the God whom we cannot see and the neighbor whom we can see become co-partners in our love.

Let us now examine the concept of love in Scripture and its relation to Jesus' message of the kingdom.

Love of God and Neighbor in Scripture

The Old Testament's understanding of love (the Hebrew word *ahab* and its cognates) covers as wide a range of meanings as our English word "love." *Ahab* basically means a voluntary attachment. Then it extends to objects or abstractions, sexual attraction, the emotional side of love, family attachments, preference, popularity, a slave's feeling toward a master, the Israelite mandate to love the stranger, and love between friends.[1]

The Greek language, in which our gospels were written, used three words for love: *eros, philia,* and *agape*. *Eros* signifies the passion of sexual desire (erotic love) and is not used in the New Testament. *Philein* designates primarily the love of friendship. *Agape* originally meant satisfaction, sympathy, or a hospitable spirit and, though rarely used, came to designate the unique and original idea of Christian love.[2] In English today, the less used and more rarified word charity is used to translate *agape*. Our liturgical song makes this distinction, "Where charity and love prevail, there God is in our midst." The careful selection of words expresses our attempt to render clear the Christian concept of love and its responsibilities. But no semantic definition of love can contain the breadth, height, and depth of its experience. For the Christian, the content remains defined by the Jesus Event that sets the norm for our love. We structure that content in our lives today, and this is what makes us Christians.

Let us first treat love as found in the Synoptic Gospels. Love of God and neighbor depend on the prior assumption that God is in fact lovable and loving. God cares for us. For our part, we find our true selves in loving God and what God cares about. In addressing God, Jesus uses the intimate *abba* (dad), which implies

[1] *See* McKenzie *Dictionary of the Bible* (Milwaukee: Bruce Publishing Co., 1965) 520.

[2] *The Interpreter's Dictionary* 3:169.

a deep fellowship of understanding and affection as well as obedience. Jesus is the beloved son and loves his father; he lives in this love relationship and shares it with others. The disciple also calls upon God as *abba*. We are invited into the same familiarity Jesus had with "our Father."

Jesus says that love of God and neighbor is the greatest commandment of the law (Deut 6:5; Lev 19:18; Matt 22:34-40; Mark 12:28-34; Luke 10:25-28). The two commandments are placed on an equal plane; and it is precisely in this equality that the Christian revolution of charity consists. Only Luke goes on to ask "Who is my neighbor?" in the story of the good samaritan. "Neighbor" in the Old Testament is commonly used to signify those to whom one is near, those with whom one lives and deals habitually.

The command to love our neighbor does not depend upon the attitude, behavior, or friendliness of the neighbor. As God loves the sinner too, and sends the rain upon the just and unjust, so we find our warrant in God's love. To love one's friends is praiseworthy and real discipleship, but others do the same. To love one's neighbor even if he or she is one's enemy is unique to Jesus. To love one's enemies implies a ground, a source, a warrant that connects us, so that to break this link, even to an enemy, causes a breakage in one's self too. That ground which supports both one's self and one's neighbor, even one's enemies, is God.

This call to love is neither absurd nor naive. It reveals a profound and fundamental truth that is also vitally important to God and neighbor. Love's command expresses a way of living that continually calls one to love more and more. It is the way of Jesus and those who follow him.

Gratitude is important to Christian love. Christians acknowledge everything that God has done for us. Every love seems to come upon us in a manner in which we are not worthy. Why should another care for us, love us more than we love ourselves, take us for who we are and not what we do? Our realization is that this love is a gift. Disciples can only open their hands to receive it and say "thank you." It cannot be merited or requested, only freely given. Gratitude recognizes that we are different, happily so, and that the change was a gift. In Mark and Matthew the opening words of Jesus call us to repent and believe the good news. Luke (7:36-50) emphasizes the relationship to gratitude when Jesus dines at the home of Simon the Pharisee. A woman, called a sinner, washes Jesus' feet with her tears and wipes them with her hair, kissing them and perfuming them with oil. She does so because of her gratitude. Then Jesus connects gratitude with love: "her many sins are forgiven because of her great love." Genuine love stems from the recognition that we are gifted by God, and it extends in Godlike fashion to others.

On the negative side, self-righteousness, so prevalent in every age, seals us up in a steel container and makes us untouched and untouchable. When we are self-righteous we harden our hearts and revel in our condemnation of others. Jesus often rails against this pharisaical position as incompatible with love. The result is seen early on in Mark (3:6) when the Pharisees and Herodians band together in a plot to destroy Jesus.

The family images used by Jesus in the Gospels are significant. When Jesus is told in Mark that his mother, brothers, and sisters are looking for him, Jesus replies that those who do the will of God are "brother and sister and mother to me" (Mark 3:35). This statement also reveals that God is a Father to us all. Love is all-encompassing and is grounded in God. Therefore it must be greater than the love that one gives to parents or to children (Matt 10:37). After the resurrection in Matthew and during the Last Supper in John, Jesus addresses his disciples as "brothers," indicating a new relationship, one that all disciples share today.

God's love goes beyond family; it belongs to all creatures. He clothes the grass and feeds the ravens (Luke 12:22 ff.); he makes his sun rise on the evil and the good, and sends rain on the just and the unjust (Matt 5:45); the least sparrow does not die without God's knowledge, and the very hairs of our heads are all numbered (Luke 12:6-7). These examples also express the intimacy of divine love for us, from the inside out as well as the outside in. We are immersed in God's love. Our ecological environment is also a gift and an expression of love.

Jesus' mission is one of love derived from the image of the Servant of the Lord. Jesus came to seek and to save the lost, to heal the spiritually sick, and to do wonders among people as one in whom and through whom the Spirit of God was at work (Mark 1:10, 23 ff.; 2:17; 10:45; Luke 7:22; 19:10). The entire life of Jesus is a story of love seeking and finding its way in the lives of human beings. As with Jesus' mission, so with the disciples: we love God with all our heart, soul, mind, and strength, and our neighbor as ourselves even to the extent of loving our enemies.

Let us now look at love in John's Gospel. Love pervades all discipleship, yet love language is much less common in the New Testament than one would expect, and one-third of the references to love occur in John. Jesus loves his disciples to the extreme (John 13:1) and lays down his life for them, which is the greatest proof of love (John 15:13). The love of God and Jesus for humankind demands a response, one that shows itself in deeds. The chief work of love is to keep the word of God and the commandments of Jesus (John 14:15, 21, 23; 15:10). The chief of the commandments of Jesus is that the disciples should love one another (John 13:34 ff.; 15:17). They should do this with the same selfless, total love Jesus showed for them.

The distinctive force of John's conception of Christian love lies in its being communicated from the Father through the Son to all the disciples who share it with each other. Jesus loves the disciples with the love which the Father exhibits toward him (John 19:9). The Father loves the Son and puts all things at his disposal (John 3:35). The Son shows his love of the Father by his obedience (John 14:31). The Father loves the Son because the Son lays down his life (John 10:17). The one who loves Jesus loves the Father, and the Father and Son abide in the one who loves Jesus and keeps his word (John 14:21, 23). A community abides in God through the mutual love of its members.

An intertwining of persons and journeys occurs in John. Disciple and master share the same fate because they are under the same obligation: to love one's life is to lose it (12:25, cf. Mark 8:35; Luke 14:26; 17:33). Jesus is our example (John 13:15). Distinctive in John is the mutual love of the Father and Son, and the paradox of the Son's obedience as the authentic mark of his divine glory. The deepest meaning of Jesus is "my beloved Son."

John's unique contribution to Christology is the doctrine of the incarnation of the Eternal Word or Logos.[3] The relations of the Father to the Spirit and the Spirit to the Son are all to be subsumed under the concept of love. Love has taken both a human

[3]Ibid., 3:177.

face and a human voice in Jesus of Nazareth, for the sake of us, the scattered children of the Father. Love reached down from God to humanity, so that humanity might rise up to enjoy life in God forever.

Jesus never advised reasonable self-love as the yardstick for neighborly love, nor love as a policy which ultimately promotes the ends of the self; for example, to be loving so no one will dislike you. Instead, sacrificial love forms the pattern of those who will serve God. This love is not the convention of race, sex, and culture. It requires a universalized heart that goes beyond the shelter of those who love us.

The message of Jesus fits within the one who sent him to us. Let us now examine its meaning and implication for our relation to God and Jesus. We will explore this systematized wholeness through our contextual-relational method, the triad.

The Triad: God, Jesus, Us

From God's perspective, love of God is the fulfillment that we seek. As Augustine said so well, "Oh Lord, we are made for Thee and our hearts are restless until they rest in Thee." We are made to find our deepest relationship in God. We are offered that relationship even now in our lives. Every human person receives the same offer. God does not force himself upon us but in a gentle way, where his splendor is seen in a mirror darkly, he invites us to this love. Why are we in this world? We have no idea finally. We find ourselves here and we respond, thereby discovering who we are and who others are.

The Christian love of God and love of neighbor go hand in glove. God asks us to find in one another our lovableness. If we cannot love one another whom we can see, how can we love God whom we cannot see? As I said above, why we have this world is not altogether clear. What we can know is that the meaning of this world has a great deal to do with loving God through loving one another. The great "test" is not that we have the same religion or the same doctrine, but that we love one another. It is as if we can only come to know and love God in this world by entering into this love of one another. For those who do, salvation is theirs.

From the perspective of Jesus, the love of God and love of neighbor come together. As human, no one loved the Father more, had as intimate a contact, or was so faithful. What were the consequences? Jesus embraced all human beings. No one was outcast, no one hurt, no one alienated, no one too small or insignificant. We can only exclaim that Jesus loved with the heart of God!

As God-made-flesh Jesus showed us the power of God's love, a love that never cringed in fear, swerved because of peer pressure, or altered because of accusations which brought death. Love in Jesus flowed out and over all, reconciling others, and showing them the very heart of God. When the Pharisees and Herodians (Mark 12:13-18) wished to corner Jesus before his death, Jesus was honest, did not bend to public opinion, and did what was right. The authority of Jesus, so powerfully portrayed in all the Gospels and a clear challenge to all other authority, comes from this all-consuming love. The authority of his action came from no more magnificent source than God's own self. Jesus spoke and lived and died in God's love for us. He was the savior of the world. His death is the saving act of the world.

For us, love centers who we are as disciples. We follow not a law but a person. Jesus becomes the one who shows us the Father, tells us of the relationship that is truly of God and not someone else, and shows us the empowerment of that love and its resulting happiness. Jesus does not restrict our responses; on the contrary he opens us to many different responses. His mansion has many rooms, and much room to be loving.

Those who follow Jesus become disciples. Those who profess to love in imitation of Jesus become disciples. Those disciples cannot live for themselves but rather, as Jesus did, live with a consuming love for all. No one is small or insignificant. The extent of this love goes even to those who hate us as enemies. In other words, no one, and no situation, can be outside the boundary of love. This is what it means to be Christian.

Retrieving Love for Today

In theology, love is the free fulfillment of the self that orients one's whole life. It begins and continues in acceptance of God's free and absolute self-communication. The greatest symbol, understanding, and expression of this self-donation is love. God's love is freely given to us, is gracious, and involves us in a continual, developing relationship of love. We conceive of this love as personal, the greatest expression of our selves and a great compliment for humans to bestow upon God. God meets us at our most human center. Responsive and initiating, this back and forth movement of personal communication is love itself. We are participants in this relationship, creating and making love present through our deeds and actions. Unlike a suitcase that we pick up and carry along, only to put it away when we wish, love is never "just another thing to carry." It is constitutive of all that we are and do.

Yet love comes to terms with its limitations: of the self, of the beloved. Disillusionment, loneliness, alienation, pain, and isolation accompany all love relationships. They represent the cost of love and indicate the total risk involved to make this love occur and keep it going. We even see God in these roles, having these characteristics. When we think about it, God must cry over the deaths of innocent people, feel left out when hatred and vengeance reign, and be frustrated at our continued lack of freedom. Of course there is a positive side where God rejoices in us, finds delight in us, melts at the sacrifice shown, and exults in the goodness of people like a proud parent in his or her children. I wonder what God must see during Easter week each year when so many hundreds of millions of people exalt and glorify God in the Jesus that was once spurned and killed. God's heart must melt to think and know that Jesus was heard, that love has won, that people have heeded the message.

Christian love indicates the way all disciples are to live. We each must specify this love in our context, with the people, family, events, neighborhood, business community, and society within which we live and by which we touch other people, cultures, and societies. Let us examine some of the challenges to which love calls us.

Life, Liberty, and the Pursuit of Happiness

LIFE

Life finds its purpose in God. The ideal is a loving person, a person-in-love. This love is not any kind of love but love as Jesus showed us in words and deeds. Disciples champion life in all its forms. In the United States, we can see where life is cheap and often threatened in its survival. A consumer society as a model makes people commodities which are bought and sold, used and discarded according to need. It threatens the unborn, the aged, and those who can contribute nothing to the society either economically or personally. These are the poor. Discipleship calls us beyond being "do gooders" who help the hurting, aged, or poor, and who hold to the principle that life is sacred for the unborn and give people pregnancy information and counseling. Love for life must go even deeper in our society, all the way to the root causes. For example, the causes of poverty are many. Most poor in our country are children. Single parent households are seriously destitute. Eradicating the causes is also an act of love.

By examining where love is not, or the negative side, we sometimes recognize more clearly what needs to be done. One area of our society that needs attention is its violence. In my travels, it has been a revelation to me that other societies regard the United States as a violent nation. Our guns, television crime and real crime, militarism, business, and political policies are aggressive and violent. Even our national symbol is an aggressive eagle of prey, while India's is a nurturing cow. Violence against people is a violation of all life.

A person can do violence to another in many ways. The physical way is the most obvious—such as beating or killing another. Less obvious and sometimes even more violent are the psychological, emotional, or spiritual ways of doing violence. The story of the great Zulu chief, Shaka, in the nineteenth century is that he thought little of killing a thief, yet found the English imprisonment system too dehumanizing for words. To control another by the use of fear, anger, or the withdrawal of love is an example of psychological and emotional violence. To threaten God's eternal punishment and damnation upon others in order to control them is spiritual violence. These examples indicate an abuse of power over another's life. The right to life is being invaded and violated.

Structures and systems also violate people and are acts of violence. Armies of one country amass troops on the border and threaten the security of another country. Economic policies do violence to others, even exacting raw materials or labor for unjust prices. Such acts threaten the life of the people who rely upon their nation's livelihood. Hence, along with personal rights that demand justice be done to one another, shoulder to shoulder stands the right to social justice.

We could extend the responsibilities to curb violence one step further to include our natural environment. Nature, creation, the blue sky, water, and clean air that we require as human persons to live must be protected. It may require a change in our consciousness to treat nature not as something to be dominated and subdued but as something to be appreciated and lived with. Nature was around a long time before human beings and does not need to be dominated. Rather, a mutuality of power, which requires a different relationship between nature and human beings, might be a better model, allowing domination to yield to cooperation.

Christian discipleship requires a love that does justice to individuals and the social structures and ecology upon which we depend. The disciple desires to love God and neighbor by touching and then permeating every dimension of human living with human loving. The goal is a world whose energy is love. This goal is nothing less than the kingdom of God.

LIBERTY

The choice to love God and neighbor in every dimension of human living is our free act. No one can make it for us. Discipleship invites us in the innermost depths of our selves to choose life by choosing love. But loving never comes on its own. Love involves "another," whether a person, a country, or nature. The disciple finds the other in God. We come to God through others but once we come to know God's love for us we are turned loose in a new way to love everyone and everything. Our love extends over all, through all, in all. God makes that possible by unconditional love for us and others.

It is truly in our love for God that our love for neighbor grows. In a world of violence, war, poverty, hunger, hatred, and mistrust, the reasons for not loving abound. In God's love for us, we find reasons to love. And in so doing we receive a vision of people everywhere as brothers and sisters. This vision is our goal. Its scope is social, political, and cultural: nothing should prevent our loving one another as brother and sister.

I have heard many people remark that a gift of billions of dollars from the United States to other countries is perplexing, a military budget of $300 billion a year unthinkable. Why don't we help the needy people here? Why do we squeeze the poor for money and support non-Americans? The money seems to be connected to other countries receiving military armaments—which is good for our defense industry—or buying products which help business interests.

The question is as disturbing as it is perplexing: is this government money of the taxpayers really supporting business ventures? Does it go to the people in some way? Is the United States foreign policy really so altruistic? Most American foreign policy is rejected and hated by people of other countries because it seems to serve only the United States' interests and those of often acknowledgedly corrupt governments. Most American citizens have little idea who we are funding, why, and to what extent. Our house on foreign policy is not in order. The Iran-Contra scandal was only one of many in a history of scandals. In the final analysis, until the taxpayer asks for accountability, it will not be forthcoming. Accountability is the first step in responsibility. We should ask for it not on political grounds but on moral grounds. The disciple may not be the most informed strategist on foreign or domestic policies, but the disciple can be knowledgeable about the violation of Christ-like values.

Whether at home or abroad, political policy cannot be self-serving. Likewise, social policy cannot accept the benefit of a few over the benefit of everyone. Nor can cultural symbols and values be used to separate people into opposing camps that refuse to speak to and learn from each other.

In a global world that shrinks each day because of our information systems, we are neighbors, or as Luke says "near," more than five billion people! Our love of neighbor has taken on proportions Luke never envisaged. To love as modern disciples is a global challenge and requires a global responsibility.

When we vote in elections, take part in business transactions, associate with other people, and voice our support or our outrage, we either bring a love of neighbor or we do not. Strategies with regard to policies may be many, but the basic motivation cannot vary. That motivation is love.

PURSUIT OF HAPPINESS

We like the right to act without constraint. The privilege of voluntary association describes an important American characteristic that is part and parcel of our freedom. Schools are a case in point. If people wish to run their own schools, they may do so; they must only find people who will volunteer the money. No one is forced to belong to an organization or even to vote; all institutions depend upon our voluntary cooperation and support. This strain is very deep in our historical pursuit of happiness. Organizations form for the purpose of consolidated action by a group. But they are voluntary. No one can make us join a group. It is our privilege to say yes or no.

Although we depend upon volunteers, we recognize that some people may prefer not to volunteer. People are not required to give their reasons or explain their actions. Everyone is free to act or to not act. However, this attitude presents a problem to discipleship: no one can love for me, I can only do it myself. The "not becoming involved" syndrome comes headlong at us when we consider volunteering. In cases of injustice, hatred, dishonesty, corruption, we *must* stand up and be counted. These evils must be resisted to fulfill the Christian message. The voluntary aspect comes only in the strategy. Perhaps, then, it might be good to consider which organizations I volunteer my time to and for what causes.

Students almost unanimously agree that one problem about volunteering is that they are already over-extended, juggling many demands at once. We do have many demands. But sometimes I take refuge in the demands so that I don't have to face other and perhaps more challenging commitments. Selectivity is a needed modern virtue. I might ask, "Which are the important causes that deserve my time?" "Which causes, even if not my cup of tea, deserve to be supported?" Sometimes people find it helpful to sit down, open up the appointment book for the last month or year, and look at where their time actually went, rather than where they thought it went. Is the bulk spent socializing at a club or working for a service organization? Are we so extended with a group that we are compatible with that we never go beyond it? What values are being upheld? Reflecting on questions such as these indicates where our time goes and where our values lie. Then we must choose to act. This discernment process will not take away the juggling act of demands, but it will put our time squarely behind our values as disciples.

If people do not know what organizations might be helpful both to themselves and to others, they can begin by contacting local parish offices who know the organizations that operate in the parish. For more information, they can call the diocesan offices in the phone book. Asking people who belong to organizations is another way to find out what they're about. Either way, one phone call can put a person in touch with their possible options. Calling others to help is also a good way to invite wide participation. The choices are up to us. We cannot do everything, but we can do something. The quality of our love for others is at stake. Time is money, the saying goes, and we know it is true to an extent. But for the disciple, the phrase becomes time is love. We want to use it well.

In summary, many ways of loving action exist. To love and thereby become a person in love is the call of discipleship. Love applies to persons, society, and nature. There are no exceptions to where love goes. The desire and ability to love all come from our love of God. God's love defines us as brothers and sisters to each other. Considering the consequences of love, we can always start with what love is not, or the negative side of life. To reject violence that oppresses persons is a loving act. We can certainly agree on that and begin there. How we go about loving will require a free decision to volunteer our time and services, usually through participation in an organization which extends and enlarges our personal contribution.

I can't help but reflect that if Peter, James, and John visited us today they would find the work of discipleship so very different from what they encountered two thousand yeras ago; not in its core but in its unimagined challenges.

Further Considerations

1. Personally: Whom do I love? Whom do I find difficult to love? Who finds me difficult to love?

2. United States Context: Where are the places of hatred in our society? Who are the people with no voice, power, or place in our society?

3. Global Context: Where are the places of hatred in our world? Who finds the United States difficult to love? What role would we like to see the United States take toward other countries and the world?

4. Church Context: Where are the areas of hatred in the Church? Where are the signs of love? How could the Church witness to love of God and neighbor in American society? In the world?

CONVERSION: THE CALL TO DEVELOP, CREATE, AND CHANGE

The message of Jesus that the kingdom of God is close at hand requires our love of God and neighbor. How we love others, subduing the antagonisms apparent to both parties, requires a conversion that lets us see people for who they are and not for what they can do. Function gives way to person. To see ourselves and others as God does is an act of humility that requires wisdom and calls us to change some preconceived notions. I don't know of any more blatantly preconceived notion of person than the concept of race I experienced in South Africa. People were color, and little more. Official registers recorded color, not people. Voting was restricted to color, not people. One white man said that if he died and went to heaven and found that God was black, he'd just as soon not enter. To enter the kingdom of God in love requires breaking our favored prejudices in order to listen to the truth given by others. It requires conversion and change.

"To be human is to change and to be perfect is to change often." These words of John Henry Newman in the nineteenth century reflected the modern world that was being ushered in, a world that we have inherited. Since Newman's time our world has become more intertwined through instantaneous information on radio, television, telephone, and computers. Likewise the world has become more interrelated through business and commerce, with the entire world relying upon other countries for goods, services, markets, and security. If the cost of a barrel of oil rises one dollar, everyone around the world feels it when they purchase gasoline. This world has also become more involved: we have become our "brothers' keepers" to the extent that knowledge and opportunity create responsibility. We have become responsible for one another: we share a common ecology of water, air, earth, and space, common survival that nuclear weapons threaten, and common causes such as justice, peace, and well-being.

Not only on the worldwide level but also on the personal level, we change often. Psychologists like Erik Erikson tell us that the personality develops through the acquisition of ego strengths, such as trust, purpose, competence, love, and care. Biologically we are most aware of our bodies and emotions changing. Socially, the statistics indicate that people now change jobs more often. Medicine tells us of changes we need to make in living habits—cigarette smoking, cholesterol intake, diet, and stress. Life's habits also force changes, for instance when we have heart attacks, mid-life crises, breakups of marriages, deaths. In a true sense, we spend much of our lives changing, whether our looks, life style, personality, or social relationships. More than Newman ever experienced, change is commonplace in our thinking today. But is there any point to all this change?

Although the Gospels did not use the specific word change, it is basic to Christian life. The Gospel use the word conversion. The process of belief depends upon our turning to hear and then follow Jesus. Because every Christian must hear and respond, conversion is constitutive of discipleship. The first words that Jesus preached were: "Repent and believe the good news" (Mark 1:14). Change, or conversion, is central to the meaning of discipleship as it continues today. What, then, is Christian conversion as Jesus proclaimed it?

Conversion in Scripture

God calls all people to enter into communion with him. God invites us to a personal relationship that extends outward to everyone and everything that God cares for. The response to the call of God requires no less than a total commitment of self, leaving behind anything that is not of God. What is not of God we call sin. When one turns away from sin, then one turns toward God. Turning to God, so as "to lean on God with all one's weight," is the act of faith. Repentance and conversion describe the initial and continual act of faith. Repentance describes our free rejection of sin; and conversion expresses our free embrace of a new way of life.

In Christian history, as the notion of sin deepened, the vocabulary that expressed the fullness of repentance and conversion did too. In the Greek bible, conversion *(epistrephein)* means a turning or returning. The physical meaning is turning in one's track and going in a new direction. The Old Testament uses the term frequently; but the noun is found only once in the New Testament to refer to the "conversion of the Gentiles" (Acts 15:3).

Conversion to God is more than a change of mind, more than undergoing an experience; it is a concrete change to a new way of life, as the word "turn" suggests.[1] One "heads in a new direction."

Although the Old Testament used conversion occasionally to refer to God's turning toward humankind, the New Testament speaks of humanity turning to God. The most characteristic use is to describe a human person's turning to God. It often is associated with "repent" and "believe," or with some turning from darkness to light, from idols to God, from vain things to a living God (Acts 3:19; 15:19; 11:21; 14:15). The emphasis is therefore upon a complete or total change in a person that can be seen in actions which form a pattern of life. Conversion is not simply outward deed, for which the Pharisaic teaching was repudiated (Mark 7:6-23). True turning to God follows upon repentance and belief, and it leads not only to an observable new way of life, but to a spiritual transformation.

The word *metanoia* from the Greek means "a change of mind," but in the scriptures indicates a change in the entire person. It includes an interior, intellectual change, but that change must also be shown exteriorly (for example by confessing one's guilt or fasting) (Jer 8:4 ff.; 31:18 ff.; Ezek 18).

John the Baptist called for conversion and repentance in a "baptism of repentance." He warned that God's judgment would fall upon all who did not comply. Jesus took up repentance and conversion in his own terms at the beginning of his ministry (Mark 1:15; Matt 4:17). Jesus came to "call sinners to conversion" (Luke 5:32). That one becomes aware of one's sinful state is an essential

---

[1] *The Interpreter's Dictionary,* 1:678.

aspect of the kingdom. A relationship with God is essential for human fulfillment. Jesus was not content merely to preach the kingdom of God; he began powerfully to make it a reality. With him the kingdom is inaugurated, although it is directed toward mysterious fulfillments.[2]

Repentance indicates that something is wrong. One is thrown out of kilter, destabilized, off balance. The need to redress the wrong is simultaneously a recognition of what it will take to get back on track, stabilized in self and relationships, and in peaceful harmony.

Conversion describes the process of moving toward that harmony. For the disciple, the purpose of conversion rests ultimately in God. Our need to change is the need to find God in every aspect of ourselves and others. One who becomes aware of his or her sinful state can turn confidently to Jesus, who can forgive sins (Matt 9:6) and bring us to peace with God. Self-sufficiency, attachment to riches, proud assurances, and hardness of heart work against that peace.

In the changes brought about by his miracles, Jesus seemed to distrust showy displays. Perhaps his own experience of being asked to perform miracles for the sake of miracles, and not because of faith, sensitized him to the misunderstanding that accompanies showy displays. In Mark especially he continually tells people not to tell anyone of his miracles. Scripture scholars called this pattern the "messianic secret." To a lesser degree, it can be found in the other Gospels. In other miracle accounts, the human ordinariness presents a shockingly strong contrast to the extraordinary change just effected. For example, when Jesus cures Peter's mother-in-law, she simply goes about her hospitality of waiting on them. When Jesus raises up the young daughter thought to be dead, he tells the parents to give her food. What matters is first the change of heart that makes one become like a little child (Matt 18:3), and then the continued effort to "seek the kingdom of God and his justice" (Matt 6:33).

The parables also bring out the act of conversion. The prodigal son (Luke 15:11-32), unique to Luke, is the best example. In ad-

[2]Xavier Leon-Dufour, *Dictionary of Biblical Theology* 2nd edition (New York: The Seabury Press, 1973) 489.

dition, Jesus' actions consistently welcome sinners, which scandalized the Pharisees, but effected conversions (*see* in Luke the sinful woman 7:36-50; and Zaccheus 19:5-9). Even to the end, on the cross, the "good thief" (Dismas) asks and receives forgiveness (Luke 23:39-43).

Let us now bring conversion into its various relationships

The Triad: God, Jesus, Us

From the perspective of God in this relationship, or at least what we can tell about God from our perspective in the light of Christ, conversion means that God expects us to change. He did not make us forever unchangeable. To have freedom implies that we can make decisions, some better and some worse, and then make others correct or enhance or continue the good decisions that we make. For example, when we find that lying does not pay off and that telling the truth no matter what the consequences gives us our integrity, then we make the choice to tell the truth. Each time we are faced with the choice, though, we have to remake our decision to tell the truth. Hopefully, over time, telling the truth will become a habit with us (a virtue). The principle of telling the truth will become so solidified in our life that it will be a basic option by which we live, and a pattern we continue through additional choices. A virtue is a habit built up from good choices. As human, we cannot keep reinventing the wheel of our deepest life choices; basic ones are formed and others cluster around them. Sometimes this basic choice for God is called "a fundamental option for God in my life." One's main values become set in one's character and the individual can get on with living. This core of choices represents our commitment.

God asks for this basic commitment in our lives. As we make choices in our world, mistakes happen. "To err is human" we say, and perfection belongs to God alone. No one goes through this life without mistakes. Sometimes the mistakes are due to our need for more knowledge. We learn more about ourselves, others, and even God as we go through life. With good advice, wise counsel, and a discerning heart, we hope to avoid mistakes, certainly irreversible ones that harm us and the world around us. A good motto for us to live by is one put forward by the theologian of conversion, Bernard Lonergan: "Be attentive, be reasonable, be responsible, be loving, and if necessary change."[3] Wherever and whenever God leads us, the disciple follows. Change for its own sake is not a consideration. Openness to change means an openness to change direction in order to stay with God.

From the perspective of Jesus, conversion is an integral part of his message. In Mark 1:14 his first words are "Repent and believe the good news." Throughout his ministry, Jesus worked to soften the hard-hearted so that love could enter them in many of its forms: compassion, generosity, forgiveness, self-renunciation, service. Jesus expected changes, often met intransigent resistance, and spoke highly of those who did change.

Change is never for its own sake. It transforms the person because he or she lives with another personal reality called God. In, with, and through God we live united. No longer is it "I" but "We." The creative interchange between God and the self is the life of grace. God abides with me through the Holy Spirit, and I try to make decisions united with God. Connected with God in grace (God with me), I act to love as Jesus did which is symbolized in the kingdom of God made present. God enters the world in a salvific way when people are fed, clothed, cared for, reconciled, loved. Contrary to what people sometimes think, being a Christian is really not complicated.

When the creative interaction with God vindicates itself, people begin to see things in a new light, new ways of being in the world occur, hope is rekindled, dreams are unleashed. This change brings with it the overwhelming knowledge that one can never go back to what one was, the way one lived, the answers one accepted. Something new and unexpected, fresh and beckoning, overwhelming and fascinating, vital and mysterious has occurred to transform our interpretation of life itself. For Jesus this transformation in relation to God spoke of God's heart wanting it for us, luring and beckoning us to accept it, by grace we say, so that the very Spirit of God was at work. Like the wind that cannot be seen but whose effects are all clearly recognized, so too God's Spirit works with

[3]Bernard Lonergan, *Method in Theology* (New York: Herder and Herder, 1972) 231.

us and animates us to become our best selves. We have referred to this abiding presence of God as sanctifying grace—the process of God and humans working together in a holy, transforming way.

From our perspective, we fear being lost in ourselves and in our world. "Dis-ease" is sickness, maybe unto death. Trapped in our past, caught in the social entanglements of others, left without choices, we are without hope. Deep down we welcome change in many forms: a new friendship, a new love, a new experience, a new insight, a new lease on life. Yes, areas of our life exist where we find good things, good people, and we never want them to change. Mary Magdalene did not want to let go of Jesus after the resurrection, after having lost him once. Having found happiness, no one wants to give it up. Yet happiness grows and changes, deepens and calls us forever forth in new and dynamic ways. We wish to change many aspects we don't like about ourselves and our world. On the mundane level, we want to lose weight, change our appearance, go to a new city for vacation, change our pace, do something different, try new experiences and hobbies. On the profound level, we wish to rid the world of starvation, violence, killing, hatred, fear, and insecurity. Americans generally like to change and certainly have based our society on our right to change and pursue happiness in our own way.

Conversion goes deeper than change. Sometimes it means that we have to abandon some things that until now we've refused to let go of (such as our wealth, our lifestyle, our associates). Conversion is never an easy purchase like a credit card transaction or a lay-away plan. It demands my total self, *now*. It is done at risk, the results are out of our control, and it requires a commitment to a future with a changed set of relationships that will exact their own dividends.

Retrieving Conversion for Today

Let us look at the call to conversion first, in order to recognize how we are invited and how we respond. Secondly, we will examine several models that present the dimensions of conversion in order to understand the call to "total conversion."

The biblical invitation to conversion comes in three interrelated stages. The first is recognition of one's state, that, to some degree, one is estranged from God. This state can be called one of Information. The second moment is the turning to God, that one moves away from sin towards God. This state can be called Conformation. The third moment is living out this newly committed response. This state can be called Transformation. Thus, when one is informed, one is invited; when one conforms, one accepts the invitation; and when one is transformed, one lives in committed relationship to the new reality as it unfolds.

We might think of the three moments of conversion in this way. The invitation comes to me from God as information. I hear God's word, in my HEAD. Then, if I accept the invitation I conform my life to it. This commitment comes from my HEART. As I live out my committed life, it is transformed by my HANDS. The Information, Conformation, and Transformation moments describe the total conversion of the person: head, heart, and hands.

Integrity in our lives comes from unity of head, heart, and hands—in other words, from my understanding, love, and action. If our actions do not show forth our understanding and loves, then we are divided people in need of conversion. If our loves are not where our understanding and actions are, then we are in need of conversion. Life in God seems to call us at one and the same time to move beyond ourselves and to possess our selves. Continual conversion is the road of discipleship.

Conversion is one of the most important topics in theology today. Not too many years ago conversion was restricted to the act of coming to faith that results in baptism. Sometimes conversion was reserved for cataclysmic changes within life, such as Paul's conversion on the road to Damascus, or the conversion from rich to poor of Francis of Assisi, or from soldier to servant of Ignatius of Loyola. We can describe this model of conversion as one from sinner to saint.

In the last few years, however, conversion has become extended to include another model. It describes the normal, continual, and ongoing deepening of a disciple's relationship with the Lord. We might call it continual conversion. Rather than a static state of being before God, conversion is now described in dynamic and processive terms. We grow and develop in our relationship with God as we do in all relationships. Moreover, we have found new and undeveloped dimensions of life calling to be related more integrally with God. One example is our growing awareness of social sin. Another is our sin of omission—ignoring the good we should have done.

Conversion is spoken about in terms of "a total conversion." Some models of what this implies might be helpful. One model examines affective, intellectual, moral, and religious conversions, which are interconnected in the individual's conscious acts. We change our feelings—"that anger was directed to the wrong person;" our thinking—"this conclusion was wrong;" our moral behavior—"I know now that I want to be an honest person;" and our religious grounding—"God is inviting me to this suffering."

This four-fold conversion makes the point that conversion in any one area may involve the other three. For example, if a young man and woman fall in love, this reality calls forth changes in how they think about themselves (not as individuals but as part of a relationship), how they behave, and how God is acting in their lives through each other. A total turning of one's self is involved, not just a revolution in one dimension. Any obstacle in the integral process of conversion results in a conversion that is not complete. One step leads invariably to the others.

The strong point of this model is its dynamic and interrelated processes. The model helps explain great one-time conversions as well as the little ongoing conversions of daily life. In a true sense, the disciple is one in perpetual conversion to God through every event, person, thought, and feeling. Everything becomes charged with the love that transforms ourselves and our world in God.

The weak point of this model is its lack of attention to social conversion, or those relationships that surround us. Another model might complement the one above.

We are people in the middle. We have a personal and social history that we receive from others when we are born. At birth, we can do nothing about that history; but as we grow we can determine and change some of it. For example, an unloved child may become a loving parent. Or a person who learned racial discrimination from society may refuse to accept it later in life. We live with historical, social, personal, and future-oriented relationships in need of conversion.

This relational model can be imagined in the form of a cross: the leftmost tip is the background or history we inherit, the top tip is the inward dimension of self including the model of conversion above, the bottom tip is the outward dimension of society, and the furthest right tip is the forward dimension for which we are striving. This model of conversion, then, has a four-fold set of relations: background, inward, outward, and forward. We might call this the cross of reality, where we live our lives in God. For the disciple, to pick up one's cross and follow Jesus implies carrying this cross of reality. We are transfixed upon this cross of life and we bring the world to God through our loving resistance to sin and our acceptance of the salvation that lies within it.

The strength of this model is its acceptance of relationships wherein we live. It pays attention to the individual and, especially, to social conversions, in both its history and its future-orientation. The model's weakness is its omission of particular aspects of personal conversion detailed in the first model. Together they can help us understand the challenge of conversion in discipleship today, and suggest how we can live an authentic spirituality of discipleship.

Life, Liberty, and the Pursuit of Happiness

LIFE

One area of conversion we are called to today is social. It is not enough to think of personal conversion. We are people within a society that impacts us, and we impact others. The Church has asked us to look at life through the eyes of those who see it very differently; through the eyes of those who suffer from society, the eyes of the poor. This is the question of social justice. The poor wish for life and find it not, wish for opportunity and have the door shut, wish for society and are marginalized. Yet these are the ones whom God loves and society does not have time for; the ones who cry and are asked to keep quiet. The voice and life of the poor judges every society and every person.

For the last hundred years, popes have consistently called attention to social conversion. Through their encyclicals, starting with Pope Leo XIII's *Rerum Novarum,* a powerful social teaching exists. Often this area is not known. Even in 1891 Leo XIII called for limits on private possessions, challenged the rich to give to the poor, insisted that the state serve all people, called the Church to unite the rich and poor, promoted trade associations and just wages, recognized that private property is a right and creates a stable society, and encouraged just relations between owners and workers. These are remarkable calls to social conversion even today.

In 1975, Pope Paul VI in *Evangelii Nuntiandi* said that Christians cannot ignore the Church's social teachings and that they must translate them into forms of action, participation, and commitment. These are strong words that indicate the social dimension of discipleship. He also said that the Church has the duty to proclaim the liberation of millions of people: to assist the birth of liberation, to give witness, and to make sure it is completed. We need to build social structures that are more human and just and respect the rights of people.

Pope John Paul II has continued to specify the social teachings since 1979. He has called for a conversion of military armament investments into food and service investments for life, to stop the abuse of the earth through military and technological exploitation. He has asked us to develop economic responsibility within a worldwide concern for people; to work for the universal human rights as the United Nations has declared a fundamental principle; and to link our commitment to justice with peace for the world. Suggestions of how to find justice in medical, labor, immigration, and refugee obligations are included in his writings.

As one can see, the themes of social justice are crucial to all people. The specific application of these principles, as Paul VI said, belongs to the disciple to bring into action.

To think in terms of social justice, especially through the eyes of the poor, the widowed, the orphaned, the slow, the hurting, the mistrusting, and the anxious, is to take on discipleship that is unfolding in our day in a global way. Our neighbor has become the starving Ethiopian, the Latin American refugee, the war-torn Lebanese, the irreconciled Northern Irish. How we respond is not clear; that we respond is gospel imperative. While we are called to global solidarity with all humanity, we experience the same degradation in our own cities, down the street, next door, in our own homes.

We can begin where we are and change the world. To begin with, that sense of frustration that results from watching the evening news, powerless, is a positive sign in itself: it indicates that we do care. The day we lose that caring is a sad one for the world. In addition to feeling compassion, we can work for life around us: in the home, in the neighborhood, at work, in organizations, voting, in the parish. Many of these groups have outreach to global concerns. We can find others whose work we are interested in and support them. Most importantly, concern for others must be nourished or nothing will be done.

While guilt can be a healthy response to decisions of life, guilt trips are not. The gospel message does not lay guilt trips, especially the kind where "you are guilty but I am not." Motivating people by placing blame is manipulative and does not help. The motivation that is strongest is love. The gospel calls us into a "solidarity with the poor" because we are brothers and sisters to each other, and we wish to act that way.

"Integration" is an important word for us today. It expresses authenticity, wholeness, and orientation of self. It does not imply a totally put-together person without limits, sickness, sin. It means the acceptance and ability to hold the struggling and imperfect self together in the trajectory of life, entrusting all to our relationship with God. It means that we continually become converted to God in every way.

LIBERTY

In the United States, we recognize that we are in a society of rapid and sometimes staggering changes. We are a disposable society that throws things and sometimes people away. The economic markets cater to our change and resistance to change, but the markets themselves are based upon whether we buy, and so are really based upon our changes. We also find ourselves changing in little ways like new clothes, hair style, a new friend. The speed of this change is so fast that it will throw us into "future shock," shock being the body's necessary closing down to everything else in order to survive. Personality theorists like Erik Erikson describe human personalities as undergoing constant change. Change characterizes our culture. Change is both wonderful and frightening.

Who we become is tied to who others will become, and won't become. We need not worry about people who have chosen to make something of their lives. We might worry about those who want to make something of their lives but cannot. These people are trapped in unfreedoms like racist attitudes towards them, ethnocentric attitudes that rob their cultural contributions, sexist stereotypes that relegate them to a role, economic elitism which looks down at them as shiftless and lazy, and religious bigotry which looks on them as unfit in the eyes of God. To break through these unfreedoms in our lives will take real conversions, not tokenisms.

How can one change these often deep-seated attitudes of unfreedom? I suppose there are many ways, but today the emphasis is on what is called an insertion experience, where one has personal contact with others on their own grounds. To experience people's pain from their side clears the air of the inclination to stereotype. Sitting down at table with other human beings, not stereotypes, changes our perspective forever. To worship with others who are different, to eat and live with them, to share their fear of the neighborhood and crime is to put oneself in their shoes and learn how they feel. We never leave such an experience unchanged.

Programs for insertion exist in many parishes, dioceses, schools, and universities, and through religious orders. Judging from my knowledge of high schools and universities, the students who took advantage of service works drew tremendous strength and solidarity from others, and it changed their attitudes and their lives. These students became converted to a concern for others that opened up new parts of their personalities. For some students it was a tremendously important conversion experience, for others it was a slowly growing confirmation of the way of discipleship already embarked upon. These actions concretely build communities of understanding and hold out hope for us all.

The Pursuit of Happiness

The bishops of the United States have called us to listen to the gospel as it applies to our historical context, and if necessary, to change. In recent years documents have been written on racism, economics, social justice, evangelization, peace for the world, care for the elderly and the unborn. These documents challenge us to think in new and informed ways. Sometimes the words are unsettling because we have just been awakened from sleep. We are overtaken by good news, but it is also troubling news, breaking upon us from the midst of suffering humanity. We wipe the sleep from our eyes and say, "I never knew how awful that was."

These pastorals are not answer sheets. They provide the principles, the theology, the tradition, and the information needed to understand why these concerns are important challenges for us to respond to today. The pastorals try to show where God's voice is calling. Great leeway is given for our response. The particulars of living the gospel are left to us, usually with encouragement to find our own way of following Christ today. One might think of the pastorals as the best expression of the current Christian parameters for answering these questions.

Beyond the pastorals, bishops call us to new programs such as sacramental preparation in parishes. The reasons behind these calls are sound and good, and offer an opportunity for people to receive adequate preparation and understanding before entering sacraments like baptism, confirmation, and matrimony.

Parishes also ask for our voluntary participation in programs such as RENEW, giving communion to the sick, serving as readers and ministers of communion at liturgy, participating in prayer groups, and other organizations. Each activity requires some commitment on the part of the individual. More importantly, each work is an opportunity to put oneself in relation to God through acts of service. The long-standing help asked by parishes is an extension of discipleship in the Church: it is a way to serve others and an opportunity to meet God in the transforming interchange of service. Again heart, head, and hand come together in an integral conversion.

The bishops in the recent pastorals have changed themselves. These pastorals are written in rough drafts, circulated among experts throughout the Church, and then sent out to the people for their reflection and criticism. The findings are given back through committees to the bishops' conference, and rewriting is done. This change of method is a living example of the bishops themselves undergoing change on behalf of the gospel and its responsibility. The bishops not only call us to conversion but also undergo it themselves. In addition, bishops of regions often make week-long retreats with one another, praying together, and getting to know and respect one another in new ways. Many bishops have stated that these retreats have changed their lives. Their model of cooperation is not readily seen or known by others, yet it is an important conversion process of creative interchange for the sake of gospel.

Further Considerations

1. Personally: What has been a conversion experience for me? What were its parts? Where did it lead me?

2. United States Context: What areas of the United States have undergone conversions? What areas are in need of conversion?

3. Global Context: What areas in the world have undergone conversions? What areas need conversion?

4. Church Context: What areas of the Church have undergone conversion? What areas need conversion?

Theme 4

SALVATION: HOW OUR LIVES MAKE SENSE

The message of Jesus has a direction and a goal: salvation. Conversion is a change to a new direction in life, with the goal of discipleship. The whole of one's life becomes authentic through a commitment to this goal. Salvation makes sense of one's life.

At nineteen years of age I could not swim. Having taken swimming lessons, I knew the crawl, the backstroke, and the breaststroke, but I really could not swim. I was afraid of the water. A slip into a hole of a mountain creek at five years of age had left me with a vivid experience of drowning. I still remember looking up through the water to see my aunt reaching her hand down through the water to pull me up. During Boy Scouts at age twelve, having mastered the swimming strokes in the shallow end where I swam more than well enough, the military instructor at the army hospital graduated me to the advanced class in "the deep end." Told to swim across the pool as a test, I struggled along in what seemed like an ocean. Next to shore, I faltered and needed air. No help came this time, but I did make it to the side. I never went back. I made a pact with myself that I would avoid water, boats, ocean liners, and airplanes that went over water. My world closed in and was defined by land. By age nineteen I was still in the shallow end. My embarrassment more than anything else goaded me to learn to swim. Others did it, why couldn't I? I learned a side stroke which allowed me to breath normally while in the deep end. Quite to my surprise and equally to my delight, I could swim and control my breathing and myself in the water. I remember to this day the exhilaration that went through me. Fear vanished. A new-found world opened up, and with it, a power inside me. Exciting and wonderfully new possibilities of boating, water skiing, swimming across lakes, canoeing, rowing, and fishing took shape—all things I wouldn't do before. I was free! Fourteen years of fear and its stranglehold left me in a moment. A new part of me was born.

Over the years I became a stronger swimmer, and I have enjoyed the gifts that swimming provided for me. My respect for the water and its power have also grown, this time through the swimming itself, which gave me a healthy appreciation for the power of water. My ability does not change the fact that several inches of water is enough to drown a person. I have realized that control is not absolute but relative. To know how to relate to water and my limits is to know how to survive and enjoy creation.

The freedom that swimming brought me is analogous to the freedom that comes in salvation. A release of psychological bonds, an evaporation of fear, a dissolution of unfreedoms occur. These are the feelings at the tip of the iceberg. "Saving" has many other meanings.

We have time-saving devices like microwave ovens, already prepared dinners, shop-by-television or catalogues, and time-management seminars and booklets. All provide for us more time than we had before. We also have savings on food coupons for vegetables or meat, half-off sales, discounts of all kinds that save money, stamps redeemable for gifts. Savings and Loans tell us that money put into the bank today can be used for a rainy day tomorrow, plus interest. Ben Franklin, a Founding Father of our country and a hero of all trades, was obsessed with efficiency.

A saving is an exchange of some type for a bargain that provides for more than you have. We could just as easily call a saving a surplus of some type: energy, time, money, efficiency, opportunity. If something is saved, then that implies that something more is left that can be used. We know that we cannot get something for nothing, but the romantic lure of such a possibility remains deep within us, so much so that when we seem to win, we take great pride in "beating the system" or "getting the best deal in town," a deal that "no one else can match."

Christian salvation is not reducible to efficiency, yet it is indeed the "best deal a person can buy." It is worth everything that we own or possess, because we ourselves are at stake. "What profit does a person show who gains the whole world and destroys himself in the process? What can a person exchange for his life?'' (Mark 8:36-37). Buying salvation is impossible, one must live in relationship with God and then one has it. A choice for God is the purchase of happiness, peace, joy, love, and solidarity with others. This is the pearl of great price, and it is worth selling all that one has in order to purchase it. Salvation is the goal of human happiness and, as Augustine said so well, ''Our hearts are restless until they rest in you, Oh Lord.'' Our God is our salvation and anything short of embracing this God is not a bargain or saving at all, rather a waste, a loss, a check that bounces, a mortgage with no collateral.

The goal of Christian life is the future that we live toward today. We want to know what life means, what life in Christ offers, and how we can set out on this journey of discipleship. Salvation is the concept that expresses our purpose and so it is constitutive of Jesus' message.

We now turn to the meaning of salvation as Jesus understood it, and as it is expressed in the Gospels themselves.

Salvation in Scripture

The theme of salvation begins in the Old Testament with the Exodus event and continues right on through the New Testament. As a concept, salvation dominates every other explanation of God's dealings with humanity. Salvation basically and radically states that life is not more of the same, that the status quo is not correct, that one can rock the boat. Salvation implies on the one hand that all is not right with humankind, that a process toward a goal has been initiated, that setbacks occur, and on the other hand that God possesses the power to bring about the needed change, that God has demonstrated what needs to be done, and that the direction for goodness is known by us.

''Salvation,'' along with ''save'' and ''savior,'' frequently occur throughout the Bible. The word's Hebrew etymology means the possession of space and the freedom and security which is gained by the removal of constriction; ''to be broad'' and ''to become spacious'' and ''to enlarge'' are its meanings. In my experience of fearing water, I know the space and freedom and security I lacked. By learning to swim my world was broadened to include other uses of water. I now know the meaning of "salvation" in one area of my life, and this lesson extends to what salvation in God means in the rest of my life.

Salvation also translates into the theological concept of "to deliver" or "deliverance." The opposite of this act is compression, confinement, restraint.[1] Frequently "salvation" and "save" can be translated by "victory." One other important word which is used to express saving is *go al* which means "to redeem" in the sense of to recover property which had fallen into alien hands, to purchase back (such as from slavery). Soon the payment of money falls out of sight and the word becomes synonymous with "deliver" and "save." The redemption, meaning deliverance from adversity, oppression, death, and captivity, is found originally and most symbolically in the Exodus event.

The Old Testament background of the New Testament usage is not lost when the Greek *sozein,* to save, is used. There is little doubt that the Greek usage also colored the New Testament meaning. The title of savior was applied to the gods and goddesses, and later to the emperors of Rome. In some instances, it reflects the deification of the king. The use of "savior" is rare in the Synoptic Gospels and John, and is found more frequently in the later writings, perhaps because of its use in imperial cults and mystery cults from which Christians shied away.

"To save" in the Synoptic Gospels refers to healing accomplished by Jesus. Healing is a sign of the saving power of Jesus, a sign which confers a greater salvation than the health of the body. To "be well" or be healthy is a sign that sin and Satan have lost control. Life wins out over death. In Christian belief, as we say in the Mass of the Resurrection for the Dead, "Life is changed, not taken away." "To be well" is to have "well-being." We are at home with God and others, and all life is in harmony. The Hebrew word *shalom* expresses a well-being or peace that extends from the person's interior heart to the exterior world around her or him. The Zulus have an expression for this: when they leave, instead of saying "good-bye," they say "go well" *(hamba kahle).* The Spanish gives a deeper sense with its *vaya con Dios* (go with God). The human wish for one another arises from the heart. That it comes

[1] *The Interpreter's Dictionary* 4:169.

from God and returns to God is the disciple's insight. Our hearts are restless until they find their rest in God.

That God (the Father) saves is basic to the New Testament (Luke 1:47). Salvation is the work of divine initiative, moved by God's mercy and not our activity; it is a work of grace, received through Jesus Christ (Luke 2:11, John 10:9). Salvation is identical with the person of Jesus (Luke 19:9) who comes to the house of Zacchaeus; and Simeon saw salvation when he saw the infant Jesus (Luke 2:30).

Salvation in the New Testament fundamentally means the same as in the Old Testament, God's saving action in history which rescues people from destruction and assures them of the greater salvation that is to come.[2] The whole New Testament is concerned with the proclamation of the gospel which is the "power of God for salvation" (Rom 1:16).

The ministry and teaching of Jesus is concerned with the work of salvation (for example, Luke 19:10: "The Son of Man came to seek and to save the lost"). Jesus' mission concerns the lost, or the lost sheep of Israel (for example, Matt 1:6; 15:24; 18:12-14; Luke 15:3-10). The unique feature of the Gospels is that salvation is offered to sinners (Mark 2:17). For this reason the conventionally religious people and leaders were scandalized by Jesus. The righteousness of *God* brought salvation, not the righteousness of humankind. The one who acknowledged his or her sinfulness in need of God's mercy was justified, not the one who boasted in his genuinely good works. (*see* the parable of the publican, Luke 18:10-14). The people from the highways, the poor, maimed, blind, and lame are invited to the Messianic banquet (Luke 14:16-24).

The mission of Jesus is closely bound up with the forgiveness of sins. "To heal" or "to make whole" is also conveyed by the Greek word "to save" *(sozein)*. Healing, performed by Jesus, is an integral part of his mission.

Evidence exists in the Synoptics that Jesus conceived of his mission as that of the Servant of the Lord (Luke 4:18, cf. Isa 61:1: "he sent me to proclaim release to the captives, to set at liberty those who are oppressed;" and Mark 10:45: "The Son of man also came . . . to give his life as a ransom for many," which echoes

[2]Ibid., 177.

Isa 53:10-12). At the Last Supper, Jesus set himself forth as the new sacrificial offering in whose blood the new covenant was ratified between God and newly redeemed Israel (Matt 26:26-29; Mark 14:22-25; Luke 22:17-20). This Servant would not only establish a new covenant with God's people, but would also enlighten all the nations.

Salvation comes in human history by an act of God. Our salvation depended not only on the fact that Christ was willing to die, but even more upon the fact that he was willing to be born (2 Cor 8:9; Phil 2:6-7). This makes the incarnation a deliberate act by God which set in motion the life-event of Jesus. I believe that this is what John understood in the Logos. Thus the incarnation is an important event only understood in light of the death-resurrection.

The use of SAVIOR for Jesus is adopted by Luke. It begins in the infancy narrative when the angel announces to the lowly shepherds that news of great joy is here, for in David's city a savior is born. As if announcing the news to the shepherds heralds the announcement to all humanity, Jesus is the savior for all. Luke alone places Jesus in the historical context of Roman history twice: his birth ("In those days Caesar Augustus published a decree ordering a census of the whole world" [2:1]) and the beginning of his preaching ("In the fifteenth year of the rule of Tiberius Caesar, when Pontius Pilate was procurator of Judea" [3:1]). Jesus is savior for universal history. Even his name "Jesus" means "God is salvation," the name the angel told Mary to give her child. But even here we learn that Jesus is connected to all of Abraham's descendants and then to all of Adam's descendants. This heritage makes Jesus kin to all humanity. Then Luke in his genealogy tells us from whence this salvation comes: Jesus is son of God (Luke 3:38). Salvation comes from God in the person of Jesus, our savior, through Judaism for all people, all time, all places. Luke's expanding and expansive view of salvation finds a parallel in the theological geography of his Gospel and Acts of the Apostles where the good news is preached and spread throughout the known world (Rome). Salvation is being accomplished through the Holy Spirit. The good news of salvation is given to all. The Church's mission is to cooperate with this Holy Spirit in discipleship.

Because reconciliation is provided by God to humanity, so too is forgiveness and fellowship. It was God who reconciled us to himself through Christ, not Christ who reconciled God to us. God is the originator of our salvation. (In Luke 1:47 God is called "savior.") Moreover, this reconciliation is not limited to the human race, but is cosmic in scope and accomplishment.

Salvation is an eschatological reality: the new age has come already and we await its final completion. It is commonly expressed in traditional Jewish imagery of a banquet. Christians understood the Eucharistic banquet, something very holy and not talked about in detail in Scriptures nor described fully, as a participation in that final banquet. The Eucharist also proclaims that salvation is a social reality. There is no individualism in the New Testament concept of salvation.

Let us now systematize the context of the message of Jesus into its various relationships. In this way we move toward the application of God's choice for us in this world.

The Triad: God, Jesus, Us

From the perspective of God, the happiness and fulfillment of the human person, and of humanity in general, lies in God. This is well-being; this is salvation. It brings humanity to its greatness. Scripture sets the drama that through one man's disobedience (Adam's), sin entered the world. Concomitantly, through one man's obedience (Jesus'), salvation entered the world. Salvation is defined over against sin, it is true, but other models of salvation are possible: namely, salvation might have been needed even if Adam and Eve had not sinned.

The need for salvation has been part of the human race from the beginning. Salvation implies that humanity returns always to God for happiness. God provides ways to help us close this gap; for the Christian this means following Jesus. God's relationship does not stop there, however; it intertwines us with one another in love of neighbor. If we are to enter into our fullness, we do not walk alone but together. A mystery resides in this communal solidarity to salvation. The mystery of God's communal concern and social self remains. Salvation is for all and it includes the way we treat one another.

From the perspective of Jesus, salvation has come. God has broken into the relationship with us in a new and power-filled way.

Life can no longer be "business as usual." God has upped the stakes, by speaking the Word in Jesus. This insistence calls forth an equally urgent response of acceptance. Why God entered the world in this way, at this time, in this corner of Palestine, through this son of a carpenter, to this Jewish people . . . remains beyond our comprehension. That God has done it is the important news. The Jesus Event is factual. Christ is the message and gift God has given. To argue why God did it is one thing; the fact that it was done is another. "Why" finally evaporates in the face of the fact that it was done. For Christians salvation does not stop with a historic event; we verify God's gift of Jesus every day in our own lives. We know for ourselves the experience of the Apostles and early disciples because God communicates with us in the same way. That is why the Scriptures are so important to Christians: they provide the norm to understand and validate our experience of God today.

So the salvation of God has come in a special way in the person and message that we term "the event of Jesus." Jesus did not hold back the fact that God was working in this event. On the contrary he called forth others, by invitation, to come and see the workings of God for themselves. He taught openly. He refused no one. He must have had a powerful sense of God's destiny for us. What can only be Jesus' own insistence comes across in the Gospels. When people reject him and consequently God's message, his sadness is apparent.

From our perspective, we are the recipients of this good news from God to Jesus to us. This God is FOR US. God is concerned for our benefit; he is caring, wooing, solicitous, and loving. Like one who is madly in love, he will not leave us alone. To withhold this love from us would mean that he would have to deny himself.

Salvation is not a private affair, it concerns us all and God himself. This salvation is not offered by a sovereign God who makes demands we jump to answer. God's salvation works gently within the very nature of who we are. Our happiness and fulfillment, our life and liberty, are intertwined in this God. Our destiny is God's destiny. Our life is God's life. Our loves are God's loves. Working within us is a God who lures us ever gently forward, onward, to completion. This gentle touch comes from God alone. If we fail to hear the word, then the judgment is there. Our rejection hurts

God's heart. Yet God reverences and cherishes us, calling and luring us to become involved in this reality of love itself.

If help comes from one another, so does harm. We hurt each other. This is sin that destroys the possibility of love in others. As we call forth others to be their best, so too do we smother the good others want to bring forth. This world's salvation is a serious affair. We are more important and instrumental than we realize because as disciples we become co-creators with God's salvation. We are not to be our brother's keeper; we are to be brothers and sisters to each other.

Retrieving Salvation for Today

Salvation is a process rather than a single act. "To be saved" means to accept faith. God saves us. The essential act of the person is faith, which comes in accepting the gospel. In other words, salvation is identified with Christ Jesus dead and risen. Our salvation comes from a higher, more potent power that introduces salvation to us. We cannot save ourselves. Human persons, in their freedom and knowledge and love, stretch themselves seemingly beyond their skins to a beauty, a goodness, an "other," a love not our own. I have seen people in hospitals, confined to bed and unable to move, who choose to love. They seem to glow, an aura surrounds them, and I know that I have met the best the human spirit is: body dying, spirit emerging beyond confinement of skin and bone. We seem at times captured and confined to this body, but such a statement attests to the transcendence in us all.

The reception of salvation by a Christian is not conceived as a purely passive act. Christians are freed FROM sin and FOR doing the actions that salvation demands, being the persons we are called to be, living in a graced mode of being-in-the-world.

Salvation has an eschatological thrust to it. It is completed in the last judgment, the parousia, the second coming. We are ushered into that eschatological kingdom now. Our baptism is a sign and seal of the growth demanded and given. We never finish with salvation's task, which is the final victory.

The history of Israel in the Old Testament is the history of deliverance. It continues into the New Testament. It continues today especially in liberation theologies, which include the structural or social environment that is needed to free people. They too hold the Exodus event in a special way, know the meaning of boundaries and oppression, and strive to be enlarged and freed from these shackles. As in the Old Testament, a political component to salvation comes with freedom.

The Old Testament did not make our modern day distinction between religion, politics, and society. Hence salvation meant a total one, which certainly and importantly meant protection from one's enemies, if not victory over them to insure security and peace. The role of the king was to provide this security. For the Israelites, Yahweh as king provided this security and victory. Salvation implies the existence of a savior who is God himself. The expectation of a savior grew as crises presented themselves and deliverance was necessary. God remains the savior: that God would become flesh as savior is the greatest gift of God's love to us. God comes to us.

To tell of God's marvelous love, that we are loved and must love one another, is the good news of salvation. But the event of Jesus did not stop there, indeed it cannot be stopped there in the Christian vision. The Jesus Event becomes the opportunity, the occasion, for the outpouring of the Spirit upon the world. The Trinitarian love of God breaks forth; God continues to save. Through the grace given in the Jesus Event, the Spirit of God continues to be poured out when the hungry are fed, the naked are clothed, when righteousness and mercy and justice are done, when Christlike love centers one's life and society. The reason is revelation; these are God's concerns.

Discipleship, therefore, has further demands and takes on some longer-term necessities: preserving the gospel, speaking to what is authentic, remembering the eyewitness accounts, the place of liturgical worship, the memory of Jesus alive in Christian communities, the spread of the gospel, and the developing organization of the Church. John seems to share these concerns along with a greater spirituality of discipleship, a greater identification with the person of Jesus, especially as found in the Liturgy of the Eucharist and sacraments.

The question of the end time continues to come up in Matthew, Luke, and John. The end time question is important because it really is asking the question about what do we do now, in the meantime, the interim. The meaning and implication of discipleship is tied to Jesus' answer. Luke begins the entire Acts of the Apostles in the context of this question as asked by the disciples: "Lord, are you going to restore the rule to Israel now?" (Acts 1:7). The Ascension and Pentecost and subsequent work of the Holy Spirit, gathering people into communities and spreading the good news in imitation of Jesus, flow out of this end-time longing. It is never an idle question of speculation.

The end time question seeks to provide a perspective, a context, for understanding our discipleship today. This discipleship is beautifully worked out and presented in Matthew, Luke, and John. The question remains for us in our time and seems more pertinent than ever before because we stand on the edge of a new world. We are a Church in the modern world, a global world, with a global family never before so capable of being realized. Of course this is the great question before humanity today: will WE make it as a world together? As futurists tell us, we are all travelling on the same spaceship called earth.

Contrary to the opinion of people who read bits and pieces of the New Testament and claim to know when the end time is coming, we do not know the end. God did not tell us. In the first century, not knowing the end time could only be a question of when God wanted to intervene with power. There was no question of our ending the world. In the twentieth century, ending the world is a real possibility. Little did we expect that God would trust us with the knowledge and power to destroy humanity. In a real way, we have the god-like power to bring the world to its end. This is awesome.

If we have the power to kill, we also bear the power to give life. God has entrusted to us the ability to cooperate in the saving of one another. This is not a token power, as if God did everything and we really had nothing to do with it. Loving God above all and our neighbor as ourselves has taken on tremendous proportions, with consequences we are seeing for the first time. Nuclear holocaust will take every life around the globe. Losing our atmosphere to pollution will kill us all. There will be no escape. Our discipleship calls us to use our freedom to choose life, not death. Along with this power to kill ourselves is the countervailing power to help ourselves and overcome hatred, killing, starvation, racism, sexism, and militarism.

Discipleship takes on twentieth century characteristics. If the United States has the power to use nuclear destruction, then discipleship in the United States means that we must call our country to its responsibility. With the whole world at stake, we must use our knowledge and freedom to preserve it. We must share our power by being responsible to and on behalf of the entire human race.

Luke's view of discipleship is an important model for our thinking today. Luke saw community as the symbol of the Church and the world: the rich and poor, the marginal, everyone had an investment by virtue of being born. Everyone belonged. No one could ignore the other. If this same model is used today, and I think it is one of the most important models Christianity can contribute to the world, then those with power hold that power because it comes from humanity and belongs to humanity. No one can go his or her own way. The responsibility will be held by some, but the exercise of that responsibility belongs to all. The powerless, the silent, the small people of this world all have an investment and belong in any discussion and use of nuclear weapons. And this holds for every other life-threatening possibility as well.

Discipleship in this form says that God has respected our freedom even to the extent that we can choose to cooperate by bringing the world to its correct relationship with God, or we can destroy it. Scripture never envisaged such awesome human potential for good or evil as, for example, nuclear weaponry. God has trusted us more than we imagined. We are responsible for one another. Perhaps this respect of God for us is why no end time could be given to those disciples.

If God has entrusted such awesome potential to our freedom and knowledge, it must be because the possibility of correct use is within our grasp. For the disciple, this is another recognition that love can conquer all. Love resides at the center of life, freedom, knowledge, community, responsibility. The gospel of love has not slackened over the years; it has become more poignant and pressing as the stakes got higher. Love of God and neighbor remains the source of our salvation.

To make salvation specific for the American context, we must examine the building blocks of the American temperament. How does salvation break into our busy work-a-day world?

Life, Liberty, and the Pursuit of Happiness

LIFE

"Where your treasure is, there is your heart," Jesus tells us. The theologian Paul Tillich makes the same point in a philosophical question: "What is your ultimate concern?" Another way of saying this is, if everything else were taken from you, what would you wish to hold on to until the last? A person? job? bank account? reputation? security? These questions ask us to look at what motivates our life at its deepest center and influences the little decisions that we make. For the disciple, love is the center that we choose. We may not have arrived at our goal of becoming loving people, but our desire is there. Too often we feel that we are not good disciples because we do not love as we wish we did. Love, however, is an ideal for which we strive. We may not be perfect lovers but we try. There's no need for discouragement, only more love.

Desire acknowledges that we experience love and are moving "on the way" in a journey of love that will only end when we can love no more. We are disciples of love as Jesus has expressed it, a love that is related to God and neighbor. This is life.

Love permeates my life and everyone with whom I deal. Do I choose to imbue life with love, in relationships, family, friends, work, recreation?

LIBERTY

The use of our freedom might be brought forward through a prayer exercise used by St. Ignatius of Loyola. Imagine yourself on your death bed. You look back over all your years. You remember your relationships with friends, your family, your work, the goals for which you strove, the opportunities that presented themselves. Then ask yourself, what do you wish you had done?

To see ourselves from our death bed cuts through the superficial things that we do, broken relationships, time wasted, goals left behind, experiences left undone, words we wish we would have said, people we wanted to know better, gratitude left unexpressed, and more. The death of others or ourselves means that what could have been is no longer possible. An earthly finality limits all these relationships.

If we say that we would change some things, then now is the time to get about our business. To live our lives according to our best selves is the best that we can do. A death filled with regrets is a sad death for sure; a death filled with all the love we can give is a happy, peaceful one.

I remember the story of St. Augustine, who was reading a book when he was asked what he would do if the end of the world were coming in one hour. Augustine replied that he would keep on reading the book.

To me this says that Augustine was living the best way he could. He was not hedging his bets, ready to take action in the event of death. He lived before his God and neighbor always as if it were the final moment, and so he had nothing to change. This freedom of conscience and mind is a goal for every disciple. If I were to die in an hour, what would I do?

PURSUIT OF HAPPINESS

We all spend time at some type of work. Sometimes it is a paying job, other times it is not paid and simply needs to be done for the sake of family, self, others, community. For example, we wash the clothes, clean the dishes, make the bed, fix supper. Sometimes our jobs consist of work we like to do, other times jobs are work we simply have to do. In either case, the pursuit of happiness goes beyond the job. We cannot put happiness on the back burner of the stove. Our challenge is to find love in every situation. Work is a labor of love if we make it so. We work for the family, for our development as human persons, for the Church, for society. Promotions, changing jobs, demotions, holding the same job—whatever opportunity we choose or find ourselves in—there is the opportunity to love. To recognize God present and us present to God is the ultimate act of Jesus' incarnation today. Jesus does not incarnate the divine and human today, his disciples do. Incarnational theology means that God enters into our world in a new way, heaven and earth touch in and through my love of God and neighbor.

Frustration, risk, concern, worry, gain and loss will be part of every job. These will not be taken away from the disciple who loves. The disciple, however, accepts them as opportunities to continue to love. The disciple does not equate success with God's approval—if success were the criterion Jesus would be the most abysmal failure and disapproved of by God. The disciple sees beneath success or failure the more ultimate concern of love. Often times religion has blessed the successful and condemned failure, but that is not the way of Jesus.

To take time aside, perhaps on Sunday when we participate in the Eucharist, or during the week, or once a month on a Saturday morning, and to pray about our work might be helpful. We bring our work before the Lord and pray for what it can be to ourselves, our families, our society. Whatever way the prayer moves, we bring the labors of our hands and head before the Lord and offer them to him. We ask that we might be transformed through the work into those who love as Jesus did. It is good to bring our work before the Lord in all its forms. There is no need to keep work separate, it involves much of our time and lives. To bring work before the Lord is to consecrate our work through ourselves to the Lord and to our neighbor.

In summary, salvation is a path that is travelled by love. That love is the treasure of our hearts which expresses itself in everything that we are and do. To love is to live and to live is to love. The long-range view upon what we do might be put into perspective by imagining what decisions we would like to make if we were on our "death beds." Life is precious and important. To bring the project of our life, especially the area of work, before God is to consecrate it in love. We find that God loves us beyond what we do to everything we are. Salvation is here and now. Discipleship is here and now. Love is here and now.

Further Considerations

1. Personally: Have I experienced "saving" of any kind? What brings me happiness? What do I dislike?
2. United States Context: Where do I see salvation happening in the United States? Where do I see dehumanization?
3. Global Context: Where do I see salvation happening around the world? Where do I see dehumanization?
4. Church Context: What do I find saving in the Church? What is not saving?

Theme 5

MISSION: WHAT WE DO
AND WHERE WE GO—THE TASK

Jesus preached the kingdom of God. To love God and neighbor is what God asks of those who wish to enter into the kingdom. To align ourselves with God's concern requires a conversion, a turning with and seeing the world as God sees it. The world has a purpose which is expressed in the concept of salvation. The kingdom, love, conversion, and salvation are realities that must be put into practice by the disciple. Living this relationship with God is never a privatized and autonomous act; as with the nature of love, it is a social and relational act. To be a person-for-God is therefore simultaneously to be a person-for-others. As in the life of Jesus himself, the disciple is not only called but also sent. We are missioned to God's task of love.

Military pilots go on a mission. They are sent to fly over a target and perform a specific task. Ambassadors and diplomats are sent on missions to foreign countries to patch up problems, represent a concern, deliver a message. Being "sent" begins in childhood when we are sent to the store for a loaf of bread, sent to clean our rooms, and sent to convey a message to Mrs. Smith down the street. We learn that we are the bearers of messages, information, and concerns. Humans become communication links, exchanging the information that bonds society.

A mission implies one who missions. I can be my own sender. But here we are talking about a social interrelationship between three persons: the sender, the one sent, and the one(s) to whom the one is sent. This is the anatomy of communication. To be missioned is to communicate with others: a sender, a messenger, a recipient. We are all familiar with this role in our experience. When Jesus sends us, we need to know what the message is and to whom we are sent. We recognize our role as "people in the middle," conveying a message not our own, to people who have the freedom to accept or reject what we deliver. We serve both the sender and recipient; we bridge the gap between God and others. The news we bring is "good news" although all may not find it so. As people in the middle, we accept this responsibility, sometimes reluctantly and at other times enthusiastically.

What then is the meaning of Christian mission? Or being sent by God to others? We turn to Scripture to inform us about the basic concept of mission and what it meant in Jesus' time.

Mission in Scripture

In the Old Testament world "mission" meant the sending of representatives for the purpose of conveying a message or task. As representatives of deities and kings, messengers held powers. Although Judaism, at the time of Jesus, had messengers (*shaliah* in Hebrew), they had no institutional status or missionary responsibility, and so their commission was more a juridical than a religious one.[1]

The idea of persuasively converting people from one religion to another was little known; most conversions came through political and military expediencies. At the time of Jesus, some missionary activity by Judaism was known and successful but there is little evidence that the Christians adopted any given Jewish pattern.[2]

From the beginning of Christianity, the proclamation of the gospel message went out to all peoples as a most important aspect of its religious obligation. Widespread missionary activity occurred following the death of Stephen (c. A.D. 36), and this activity was directed to non-Jews as well as Jews. Paul's mission was to the Gentiles: it was understood to be a continuation on a wider scale of what had begun at the time of his conversion, and was in direct line with Peter's mission to the Jews. The mission was understood to be universal or catholic. The redemption of Christ was inter-

[1]*The Interpreter's Dictionary,* 1:171.
[2]Ibid., 3:405.

preted to be for all people, all historical situations, all cultures. It was the mission of the Church. This mission was a public one, without necessarily implying a particular social or political style. The result was that on the one hand the mission was soon separated from Jewish cultural and religious features, and on the other hand the Church could not totally identify with Hellenistic-Roman culture and religions (Gal 3:28). Its message predominated; subsequent structures supported the mission.

The pattern of mission came from Jesus' life. As Jesus was sent by the Father with a message (Matt 15:24; Luke 4:18), so did Jesus send out his disciples with his own authority and power to extend his mission. The word "apostle" (sent) designates the twelve around Jesus but also applies to other missionaries and messengers of the Church. It is characteristic of the Church itself (it is even one of the four marks of the Church: "one, holy, catholic, and apostolic"). Jesus sends out the Twelve with power (Matt 10), as well as the seventy-two (Luke 10:1-20). Implied in the number twelve certainly is a reference to the twelve tribes of Israel, the apostles being identified as the new "tribes" who represent the entire Church. The Book of Revelation calls the Twelve the foundation stones of the New Jerusalem.

The New Testament shows that the Church was aware of the identity of the apostles as ambassadors of Christ (Matt 28:19) and the Father (John 13:20; 20:21), serving the Church (Mark 10:44; Matt 24:45-51) by founding and building up local Christian communities (Acts 8:14). The apostles were entitled to administer baptism (Acts 2:41), to celebrate the Lord's supper (Acts 20:7-11), to perform the laying on of hands (Acts 6:6), to exercise Church discipline (1 Cor 5:3-5), and require the obedience of the community (Rom 15:18). Apostles were the foundation of the Church (the Twelve form the foundation stones of the New Jerusalem [Rev 21:14]), and were witnesses to Christ, especially his resurrection. Paul claimed his apostolicity through his seeing the risen Christ.[3]

Luke preferred the designation "apostles" instead of the Twelve. The Twelve is found only once in Mark (6:30) and in Matt (10:2), which suggests that the title was not a primitive designation in the

---

[3]Cf. Karl Rahner, *Encyclopedia of Theology* (New York: Seabury Press, 1975) 967–69 by Adrian Hastings.

Church. It is not found at all in the ecclesiastical sense in John. Interestingly, in Luke, after the narrative of the seven deacons chosen to serve, Acts abandons the use of "Twelve" and henceforward employs "apostle." We see a transition in leadership and the extension of the ministry of the Twelve taking place.[4]

The apostles' first commission empowered them to expel unclean spirits, heal diseases, and announce the kingdom (Matt 10:1; Mark 3:13-15; 6:7; Luke 9:1). They were to carry on and continue the work of Jesus; to preach repentance (Luke 24:44-49), to make disciples and to baptize (Matt 28:16-20). The mission of the Twelve was rendered operative by the gift of the Spirit after the ascension of Jesus (Luke 24:49; Acts 1:8; 2).

Every disciple, then, shares the Christian message with others because it is God's good news to everyone. The Christian, in this sense, always shares in the apostolic character of the Church and so is missioned or sent just by virtue of being a believer. The modern disciple finds its mission in the same sending out as the Twelve and the seventy-two. Likewise, whoever receives them receives the one who sent them (Matt 10:40), and receives the Father who sent Jesus (Mark 9:37; Luke 10:16; John 17:8, 25). The sender, Jesus and the Father under the power of the Spirit, comes with the one who is sent.

"Serving" is a fundamental characteristic of this ministry. The ones sent are models, as Christ himself was one who serves (Luke 22:27, John 13:13-15). Greatness of the ministry comes not from outward rank but in proportion to service (Matt 20:25-28; Mark 10:42-45; Luke 22:24-27).

Jesus understands himself as doing the work of God, as being God's envoy, bringing God's good news of salvation in the kingdom. In John's gospel the sending of the Son by the Father is a constant refrain (appearing forty times), to do his will, to accomplish his work, to speak what he had learned of the Father. Jesus announces the gospel, fulfills the law and prophets, brings fire upon the earth, brings not peace but the sword, calls not the just but sinners, seeks out and saves that which was lost, and gives his life as ransom for all.

The disciples accomplish their function through the power of

[4]*The Interpreter's Dictionary*, 3:386–87.

the Spirit poured out upon them at Pentecost. That day marks the beginning of the mission and, in a true sense, the birthing of the Church that now awaits Jesus' final gathering of us at the Final Judgment. This Spirit of Jesus and the Father sends the disciples out on mission and teaches them to rely upon God as "Abba, Father" (Gal 4:6). In the mission is unfolded the mystery of the Godhead, the transforming act of returning all things back to God, and transforming humanity in the image of the sons and daughters of God.[5]

The Triad: God, Jesus, Us

From the perspective of God, there are things to be done. These projects certainly include the individual's happiness and fullness of humanity, the relationships with other people that become a society and culture, and the past moving toward the creative future. God wishes our fulfillment, integrity, authenticity, life, liberty, and happiness. God wishes the fullest extent of all good gifts for us. The reality is that all these gifts "come from the hand of God" and are related to God. Or, we possess them by possessing God. The reality is that this salvation is in process: it is here already and not yet complete. God asks us to participate in this process. We become light on the mountain top, salt that does not lose its savor, a gift to others and signs of this reality. This is mission.

From the perspective of Jesus, the urgency of God's call comes to be in Jesus. The time is now, the decision must be made, the opportunity will pass. Something new is being offered; something new is being demanded. The gospel command to love goes beyond any reasonable demand. No natural law can arrive at this command. Jesus announces the message in the name of God and follows it in the name of us. Jesus is divine savior, human brother, God-made-human, and human-made-God.

From our perspective, Jesus becomes the messenger from God and the message, norm, and model for us. The message is the Christ Event that brings the message and mission into one action or event. We are related to this event, not in any external way but in an internal way. When we follow Christ in love, compassion, self-

[5]Leon-Dufour, *Dictionary of Biblical Theology,* 368.

renunciation, and service we find God confirming our acts and simultaneously our integrity from within the acts themselves. The resulting happiness is self-authenticating; it reveals God's message as true.

We also share internally the intimacy of God's presence in our missioning. But this is not an internal pietism, we know of God's intimate presence through the effects of others and society. The Last Judgment in Matthew makes clear that God confirms his presence through these effects: people are fed, clothed, visited, cared for, freed. Jesus told his detractors to look not only at his words, whose internal authority came from God, but also his deeds, those signs of the coming of the kingdom. The miracles attest to the kingdom, the growing in faith, the reign of God present with us, and the coming of its fulfillment in the eternal banquet with God.

The mission of God always calls us forward. We can never go back. We can never sink into self-pity or narcissism. We can never irresponsibly lose ourselves in others and society. We always go forward. We change. We follow. And the missioning of us by God continues to unfold.

Retrieving Discipleship for Today

Mission is not foreign to non-Christian religions. Mohammed considered himself "the envoy of God" and Islam has always been a strongly proselytizing religion. Buddhism left India and found its strongest followers elsewhere, especially in southeast Asia and finally in Zen form on the islands of Japan. In the last century, Hinduism has begun missionary efforts in the Krishna movements. Missionary work in the Christian faith has often been synonymous with going to foreign lands. The tradition is rich with missionaries like St. Paul (Gentiles), St. Augustine (England), St. Patrick (Ireland), St. Francis Xavier (Indies), St. Bonifacius (Germany), St. Isaac Jogues and his North American martyrs, Junipero Serra . . . the list extends to every continent and country in the world. While we may not have done everything correctly, it is a glorious heritage. The mission cannot be separated from the one missioned, and most probably brought too much of a Western mentality, but we never neglected the people.

The process today is less quantitative in terms of places and numbers of souls to be saved from eternal damnation, and more qualitative in the encounter with God that is lived. This vitality is found in the cultures and their own spiritual values. Becoming westernized is not part of the gospel message. Nor is there an automatic approval of all cultural values as if they were not in need of conversion to God's love. Every culture has more than its share of oppressive structures. The challenge is, like the seed that is planted and comes up very different from its first appearance, to plant the word of God and be willing to encourage its legitimate growth through different cultural forms. The Christian Church has a long tradition of variety in its rites; it does not seek to substitute uniformity for deeper unity. The unity in the Holy Spirit is our only basis and strength.

Our mission today requires a new attention to the context of culture, society, and the particular values operating therein. Our mission has not changed, but the attention to how we preach the message has changed. It is not our message but God's. Therefore we wish to check constantly with one another about whether our preaching represents our authentic experience of the Lord.

Mission today also has been purified somewhat of its emphasis upon leaving for foreign lands. Mission is needed in our own neighborhood, city, state, and nation. Questions about how to live our lives in relation to God, find God in our daily encounters, and resist evil are always with us. Evil does not take a holiday, and neither does loving others. For disciples, mission is forever; it is a way of life. We need only to be alive to be on mission. The real concern of the disciple begins with the immediate world around him or her, and opens in ever widening circles to embrace humanity, which in turn embraces us in our locale. How do I become responsible for the mission that I have because I am a Christian?

Life, Liberty, and the Pursuit of Happiness

LIFE

The general mission of every disciple is to love. The specific way of loving, in all its manifestations, including service, reconciliation, and compassion, is the particular mission of each person. Thus a key which unlocks our mission is our availability. Are we at God's disposal? Are we available to serve God as the Lord sends us? In this situation? At this time? Availability asks the important question of every human person: Are we free? This question asks if there are disordered attachments which hold us back from God. If so, then the challenge is to find the obstacles and free ourselves from their power. To choose life is to choose that which empowers us to become our best self, and to be that person in loving relation to others.

Another way of asking if we are choosing life is to look at those whom we empower. If we empower those who are privileged, the wealthy, the successful, the famous, then the question arises whether our mission is for everyone. Privilege comes at the expense of others. The current distribution of wealth, for example, is skewed to the minority who have much and ignores the majority who have little. Roughly ninety-four percent of the world's goods are used by six percent of the people. The point at issue is to provide resources for all, so that they that can participate in life in a human way.

To even the distribution we must look at the minimal level. Who empowers the poor? In the United States the poorest of the poor are black women who are single parents. From their perspective, they find that they are triply victimized in our society by being poor, women, and black. The disciple can draw a line that does not put the poor outside human concern with such explanations that "the poor won't work," "they are lazy," "they don't want a job," or "they want something for nothing." The evidence shows that, while a very few might be guilty of such accusations, the opposite is the reality. The poor want work, jobs, do not want handouts, do not want to be on welfare. Then who empowers them? Through supporting organizations, legislation, educational and employment opportunities, disciples empower the poor. Direct help, perhaps employment, certainly is included. We can do something. To see such work on behalf of the usually voiceless and powerless poor is a necessary component of our discipleship.

LIBERTY

Discipleship is an invitation to serve God and neighbor. In our society within our world, in our families, in our personal life styles, we show forth the values by which we live. To be free is to be free FROM those areas of our lives that keep us from loving God and neighbor. I remember asking graduate students in a seminar what they thought was the greatest obstacle to Christian life in the United States. To my amazement each of the nine came up with the same conclusion: comfort. While they knew that many other obstacles exist, they felt that comfort rendered persons indifferent to love and hence to concern for others and even to any personal need for growth. Reflecting on these answers over these years, I have come to see their wisdom.

The disciple can freely choose to live a life where comfort is resisted. To live simply, that is, to live without heaping up material possessions, is discipleship. To go through clothes once a year and see what has not been worn—not because it isn't in style or because we want a new wardrobe—and to divest ourselves of this accumulation might be beneficial. Examining where our time goes, whether in front of a television set or in conversation with the children or friends, might indicate whether patterns we do not want are developing in our lives. On the other side, are we overextended, using our activities as a buffer that leaves us uncommitted, anesthetized to raising other questions? Comfort comes in many shapes and sizes, to bring some discomfort into our lives is wholesome and opens us to a critical edge, a perspective in solidarity with others. To cave into comfort is, sorrowfully, to make ourselves the mission, and not other people.

Pursuit of Happiness

Mission is not the idea that we are more special than others. We do not have something to sell or something to give. I remember my superior's comment to me on the occasion of my ordination to the priesthood. He wrote and told me that in his experience—and he thought mine would bear this out—we do not bring Christ to people so much as we find Christ already present in people. We encourage them to live this already present relationship in its fullest way. I would say now, these many years later, that his words were correct. God is working in and for others long before a disciple on mission comes. When we speak the truth of the gospel in our words and in our lives, people do recognize Christ's voice within themselves.

Our special mission changes. In this time and place, my disciple-ship calls forth other gifts. If I am in the city, at a university, business, neighborhood, or whatever, those circumstances shape my discipleship. If I am in the United States or in Africa, the context shapes my discipleship. I participate in an ongoing project of building the kingdom. To be unselfish, to cooperate, be humble, be a leader, be resistant, be forgiving, and above all be loving are the same provisions carried by every disciple, though they are used in a specific context.

We all can contribute. The disciple performs the good, loving act, and lets it shine before others. As Socrates said, "The unexamined life is not worth living." The disciple must pray and examine his or her motives and relationship with God in this context. The Buddhist would add: "The unlived life is not worth examining." We learn discipleship by living it and all our understanding goes toward the living of discipleship. The disciple concludes, "the unloving life is not worth living, and the unloved life is not worth examining." All is in God.

In summary, the mission of disciples is to empower others with the Holy Spirit of God. Love is the generic mission that we all share; the different expressions of love in every particular event of our lives comprise the *way* we love. Whom and how we empower, and the structures of politics, economics, and society that either sap or nurture this effort are the arenas wherein the disciple is responsible. Those who suffer from deprivation, especially the poor, are the first subjects of discipleship. To raise the minimal level of human life and liberty is a virtuous act of mission. What one can be is not as clear as what one cannot accept. The choice of living is ours, and the subtle temptation to be comfortable debilitates our capacity to be sent out on mission. To choose not to be comfortable is a countercultural stance which expresses our solidarity with humanity.

Further Considerations

1. Personally: What would I like to do with my life as a Christian? What would I not like to do with it?

2. United States Context: What positive directions do I see taking place in the United States? What are negative ones? What will the United States look like one hundred years from now?

3. Global Context: What positive directions do I see taking place in the world? What are the negative ones? What will the world look like one hundred years from now?

4. Church Context: What do I think the Church's most important role, message, and action might be in the United States? The world?

FORGIVENESS AND RECONCILIATION: TO MAKE ALL THINGS WORK TOGETHER UNTO GOOD

The life of the disciple is not without its mistakes. Despite our best intentions, the evil that we do not want happens. We can never think that disciples are observers in this world, untouched by evil and its sources. No, we are participants and take the risk of life, where good and evil are often mixed indistinguishably together. This reality is captured in our tradition, where we recognize that we are both sinners and saints. While not exempt from sin and evil, Christians are called to recognize their responsibility and to seek to repair the damage, whether towards a person, a relationship, or the self. Like a rocket travelling through space that if not corrected will lose its course and career aimlessly into outer space, so too do we need constant course correction. Thus forgiveness and reconciliation are part and parcel of discipleship. To continue to make all things work together unto good is an ongoing task connected with the call to mission.

Everybody makes mistakes. Most of us have been taught to ask for forgiveness. It is a basic human experience that mistakes, even unintended, do happen and that repairs have to performed because greater concerns are at risk, such as the love of the family, or duty toward the society. We all rely upon trust and honesty in a relationship. If that trust or honesty is broken, then the relationship is called into question and we need to overcome the disposition not to trust another again. Can the trust relationship be restored after a breakage? When we give another person who asks for it a chance, oftentimes the amazing result is that the person does prove trustworthy, having learned the lesson after the mistake. At other

115

times, a person is caught in the throes of a pattern in life (lying, selfishness, jealousy, negative self image) and it takes more time and trust to climb out of the entrapment.

We all make mistakes and we all need to be forgiven. Not because we made a mistake but because we value the other person and ourselves more than the mistake. Usually a mistake cannot be reversed. The other person must live with my action, and I must live with the reality that the other person need not forgive me. Acknowledging weaknesses is considered by some as vulnerability, so they hide it. Unfortunately, to hide parts of one's self often becomes the greater lie. If I do that, I live a life of duplicity and deceit, even to myself.

The Christian understanding of forgiveness is not for hiding but for walking into the light. It gives the lie to forgiveness as vulnerability and declares it a strength. In the Christian framework, forgiveness can only be a strength, because it puts my integrity and honesty back into my relationship to everyone, including my God, and declares that life cannot go forward except in integrity, honesty, and trust.

Christian forgiveness is an ideal that we all keep before us: forgiveness is infinite because it is the way God deals with us. The act of reconciliation is an entrance into the mystery of God, and the call to become truly human precisely in our human choices, breakages, failures, and triumphs. To love one's enemies is a clarion call to a virtue that few of us possess, yet we hope to be able to exercise it when we are called upon. This desire to extend forgiveness is enough for any human to hope for. Entering into this doorway even a little distance brings one into the profound mystery of Jesus upon the cross forgiving his enemies, "for they know not what they do." Could they have known that they were killing the Son of God?

Let us now examine the meaning of both forgiveness and reconciliation as Jesus understood them, because this is the basis of our current understanding.

Forgiveness and Reconciliation in Scripture

"Reconciliation" is the Greek legal term applied to the estrangement between husband and wife. Paul applies this familial term to express the process of salvation with God who is the agent of reconciliation. Christ is the means by which reconciliation is extended to the world.

Reconciliation is paralleled with ''making peace'' and, for the Christian, happens when Jesus' blood is shed on the cross. Reconciliation refers to people moving away from the state of estrangement and hostility which has resulted from their evil deeds. It also refers to the particular reconciliation between Jews and Gentiles in the one body of the Church.[1]

In the Old Testament imagery, Yahweh proposes reconciliation to his unfaithful spouse. God offers humanity pardon, freely restrains wrath, and speaks peace to all people. Israel's sins break the Sinai covenant; but far from being resigned to this, God will take the initiative to establish a new and eternal covenant.

In the New Testament, the perfect and definitive reconciliation has been accomplished in the person of Jesus the Christ, the mediator between God and humanity. Reconciliation reflects one significant aspect of Christ's work of redemption.

Paul understands that: (1) reconciliation came from divine initiative linked with the cross and the great love; (2) the effects of reconciliation are that God no longer takes account of the faults of humanity, ''a new creation'' occurs (2 Cor 5:17), and there is a complete renewal, with access to the Father (Eph 2:18); (3) the ministry of reconciliation is the entire work of salvation, already accomplished but continuing to the parousia. Thus, the continuing ministry of reconciliation takes place, we are ''ambassadors for Christ'' (2 Cor 5:19 ff.) and the apostles are ''the messengers of reconciliation,'' architects of the peace which they announce (2 Cor 6:4-13).

Paul also understands reconciliation as UNIVERSAL: (1) the world is reconciled, both on earth and in heaven (Col 1:20), and the hostile angelic powers have come to an end (Col 2:15); (2) there is reconciliation of Jews and pagans—Christ is ''our peace'' (Eph 2:14), the era of separation and hatred is over, all people form one body in Christ (Eph 2:16). Paul has been the inspired theologian and untiring minister of reconciliation, but it is Jesus who by his sacrifice has been its creator. Jesus taught us that we cannot render

[1]McKenzie, *Dictionary of the Bible,* 722.

pleasing worship to God if we do not first reconcile ourselves with our brother (Matt 5:23 ff.).[2]

The concept of *forgiveness* belongs with the word reconciliation. In the Old Testament, that Yahweh is forgiving is commonplace. Yahweh is asked to forgive because of his great love. The great context for forgiveness is love, and sin signifies the turning away from this love. Confession of sin, conversion from sin, and prayer for forgiveness are necessary conditions before true forgiveness can take place (Hos 14:3). Forgiveness of sin is one sign of the messianic future (Isa 33:8; Jer 31:34).

In the New Testament, John the Baptizer preached a baptism of repentance for the remission of sins. Jesus claimed and exercised the power to forgive sins. When challenged, he manifested his claim by the power to heal, a divine power he claimed through his Father (Matt 9:2 ff.; Mark 2:5; Luke 5:20). The faith of the petitioner was a condition. The Christian knows salvation through the forgiveness of sins (Luke 1:77). Forgiveness of sins is the work of God's patience (Rom 3:25). The essential difference between Old Testament and New Testament is that in New Testament forgiveness comes through Christ—by his own personal forgiveness (Matt 9:2; Mark 2:5; Luke 5:20), and through his redeeming death (cf. the Eucharistic formula of Matt 26:28).

Forgiveness is a free gift from God. As a corollary, Jesus stresses the duty of Christians to forgive one another (Matt 6:14; Mark 11:25; Luke 17:3 ff.). This duty becomes a condition for obtaining forgiveness of one's own sins from God (*see* the parable of the unjust servant, Matt 18:21-35; or the "Our Father"). Jesus conferred upon the Twelve the power to forgive sins on behalf of God (John 20:21-23). This can only be understood as power exercised through Jesus, a power communicated through the reception of his Holy Spirit.

Let us now gather together the meanings from Scripture and relate them in a systematic way to discipleship.

The Triad: God, Jesus, Us

From the perspective of God, reconciliation is desired. God wishes us to be united with the divinity. God wishes healing for

[2]Leon-Dufour, *Dictionary of Biblical Theology,* 480.

us so that we might be whole. Whatever keeps us from God should be overcome. Whatever keeps us from allowing God to be more present in our lives should be removed. But we may not be able to remove the obstacles ourselves. Here is where we must rely upon God to remove them. We depend upon God and his graciousness to help us even where we cannot help ourselves. Never does this dependence do away with our freedom and our responsibility; rather, it is to whom we direct them that counts. If we are receptive to God's workings, willing to let God be God in our life, then what God wishes for us can and will be accomplished. It is this childlike trust that Jesus tells us to have that sets up the conditions for transforming love. At the multiplication of the loaves, Jesus used the food given by a young boy. From this trust in Jesus, the food for the multitude was multiplied. The great nourishment by God asks for our trust, our selves in God's hands, and then great things beyond our powers of imagination happen.

God knows that things go wrong, relationships break, hurt happens, and recommitment is needed. Deep within ourselves we need to know that we are not rejected because we have tried and failed. We desire to belong to another, to be accepted for who we are and not simply for what we do or have. This acceptance is the basis of true love, between humans and between us and God. Forgiveness is a necessary condition for growth, for belonging, for continuing.

It is not that we intend to do things wrong, hurt others, make mistakes, but the fact is that we do. We then need the forgiveness that reconciles us with one another and with God. The relationship cannot return to where it was, but it accepts the mistake within the relationship and the two work to transform it into a stronger relationship. Fidelity, commitment, resolve, deeper and more appreciative love can ensue from forgiveness. People become stronger and better through these experiences.

I once logically figured out that if mistakes made me better, then I should go ahead and make many of them. My logic gave way to experience which explained that, if I did my best and a mistake happened, I could do no better. Then the real learning took place and so did the evolution of a better person. Conversely, fear of a mistake paralyzes my contribution.

God does not turn away from us. God's fidelity is forever. God's commitment to the covenant will not stop even if we break it. This consistency and open-ended and always-turned-toward-us love tells us of God's seriousness about our salvation and our need for divine forgiveness.

From the perspective of Jesus, he began his preaching with "Repent and believe the Good News." Although repentance is not identical with forgiveness, it is an act of reconciliation through conversion. The conversion and reconciliation are toward God, which brings us to one another. Jesus tells us to pray familiarly with God as *abba* (dad), to be childlike in our approach to God's workings with us, to trust in the amazing growth of an unheard of thirty-, sixty-, or one hundred-fold harvest in this relationship. We are to place all our trust in God. Jesus also tells us that to the extent that we forgive others, so will we be forgiven. He commands us to love one another as he has loved us. He tells us to forgive not seven times (a generous number in itself!) but seventy times seven. This formula means an infinite number of times, and it reflects God's attitude toward us. No thing, no one, is great enough to block the reconciling love of God.

From our perspective, reconciliation is demanding. Too many good reasons exist to *not* extend forgiveness. Too many good theories say that we don't do the other person any good by being involved. The societal street smart wisdom says to cut bait and go away. What does forgiveness get you? What is its cash value?

These worldly wisdoms look to the benefit of the individual and not the relationship. They measure and calculate the odds. Reconciliation seems foolish by these assessments. Reconciliation calls us to be better than we are; that is what makes it an important human quality. People become better through it. Just as we all need forgiveness, so too do we all need to extend forgiveness to others. Jesus tells the parable of the man whose debt is exacted of him. He cannot pay so it is reduced. The man thanks his master. Then that same man goes out and exacts a debt from another. When the other man cannot pay, this same forgiven man exacts complete payment without mercy. When the first master hears about this he brings the unmerciful debtor back, scolds him for his treatment of others, and then states, as his own wishes have indicated, he too will pay the complete amount. Jesus has told us of the inextricable bond between our forgiveness of one another and God's forgiveness of us.

Retrieving Forgiveness and Reconciliation for Today

The need for reconciliation runs deep in our world today. Wars, violence, fear, aggression, retaliation, preemptive strikes, nuclear deterrence, star wars, terrorism, revolution, oppression, covert operations, repressions, uprisings, and demonstrations are only some of the indicators of the estrangement we experience. The unity of people is not a given; it is a goal that has to be achieved. We humans find so many ways to divide ourselves; but do we work as hard to unite ourselves?

One of the greatest challenges that we face is whether we can live together in some type of human community on a fast-shrinking globe. Clinging to land on this planet as a way of defining our identity may become an obsolete practice. The land will have to be defined by humanity. Space colonies and other forms of living certainly will change our concept of ourselves and our planet earth. Even now the sacred, unavoidable survival of humanity rests with humanity itself. To treat one another as human not only in principle but in fact is already a condition for our survival. But with a history of destruction and hate toward one another, that humanity can become unified enough for survival is a great hope and not an insured reality. The need for reconciliation becomes all the more important. Who will "blink first?" Who will work toward stopping the downward spiral of violence, in the name of justice, so that we can rebind the ties that connect us?

Peter was called "rock." We so often see Peter as an apostle of faith and forget that he was the apostle who most received forgiveness. He knew what breakage in life was about, especially when he betrayed Jesus. Because of the depths to which Peter descended, he also knew the heights of love. The artist El Greco (1541–1614) portrays this well in his painting of "St. Peter Weeping." Peter clutches the keys to the kingdom against his chest, his head tilted back and tears welling up in his eyes. The line of Luke comes to mind, "He went out and wept bitterly" (Luke 22:62). Peter is resignedly calm and unashamed in this painting. One concludes that Peter would be slow to condemn the weaknesses and struggles of others. Patient love built upon forgiveness and faith make a solid rock as foundation.

Reconciliation must include for disciples the gumption never to give up. We pursue ideals, but when they break we do not need to point fingers, make people feel shame, disown people, or cast aspersions toward them. They need support and help most at these times. They do not need people to take sides or give them advice; they need people to support them. The goal is to have life rise from the ashes, to bring hope from defeat, to unleash freedom where people are captive to their own self-doubts and worthlessness. The pursuit of happiness, given breakages, is needed. It would be a great compliment to Christians to be known as those who never give up. We strive for ideals, but we are also realists who know how to accept human breakages and begin again. This is indeed a virtue for our day, and a form of reconciliation that needs to be exercised.

The development of the sacrament of penance or reconciliation resulted from Christians who had not been faithful to their baptismal commitment, primarily because of persecution by the Roman Empire. Their actions were seen as betrayal and separation from the believing community. Could people come back to the Church? The answer was an agonized "yes." Restoring the relationship was difficult. Forgiveness does not wipe clean the slate of life's deeds, but it does say, "I'm willing to not let this get in the way of our relationship. I commit myself to grow by and through this breakage."

Luke's parable of the prodigal son deals with precisely this problem. The father forgives the prodigal son for taking his inheritance and squandering it. The brother who remained at home becomes upset at the favored treatment of his renegade brother. The father assures the son of his love and tells him to rejoice because his brother who was lost is now found. The parable tells us that it is not sufficient to forgive one's brother because God did, one must also accept that brother back as a brother even if it is difficult and goes against one's grain. The forgiving attitude of the brother must become like God's. True forgiveness cannot be self-centered or self-serving, but must look only at the other person's good.

Throughout the Gospels, Jesus forgives and reconciles people to one another. The forgiveness is heard as very good news indeed. "Things can be different," it says; "we can be different than we are." A new reign can enter. Luke records Jesus' forgiveness of his executioners as some of his last words on earth. The depth of that forgiveness was not lost on the disciples. The reconciliation effected through the transforming nature of forgiveness was the sign of the cross. Heaven and earth were united in this death. Something new happened. As the sacrificial lamb who took away our sins, Jesus reconciled brother and sister, humanity and God. The high priest whose role in Judaism was to offer sacrifice on behalf of humanity, thereby mediating the relationship between humanity and God, was Jesus. He was both high priest and sacrificial offering. His sacrifice is the supreme one. Likewise, those who follow him become priests whose work is reconciliation. Christians share in the one priesthood of Jesus, mediating the reconciliation of humanity and God. We are, as Paul says, "ambassadors of reconciliation" and thereby we proclaim the meaning of the death of Jesus.

To be forgiven is to be loved. Love accepts us not for what we can do, or what successes we have, or what advantages we offer, but for who we are as people. Love casts out darkness. Not even our mistakes stand in the way of love. Mistakes are real, sometimes irretrievably harmful, but the person is never confused with the mistakes. Through forgiveness love calls forth the possibility of love once more. The conversion from sinner to saint remains in every one of our challenges.

To specify the meaning of forgiveness and reconciliation for our day, we look at the American context.

Life, Liberty, and the Pursuit of Happiness

LIFE

In the ordinary course of life, human relationships go through rocky times and sometimes break. Some can be mended, others cannot. But to harbor hate or revenge is self-destructive. To acknowledge that breakages exist, even without our intending them, and to hope for the other's good, is to take away the destructive elements of hate and revenge. Forgiveness is an act of love that regards the other as a person first of all.

Breakages happen in families. They occur between parents and children, brothers and sisters, in-laws, aunts and uncles, cousins. Perhaps most difficult is the breakage between husband and wife.

Every engaged young couple thinks they will be married forever. They generally know the statistics are fifty percent against them, nevertheless, they will beat the odds. This hope in their hearts is important, but if they do not make it, can they pick up their lives and continue on?

Divorces are never easy. Divorce is an acknowledgement that a relationship has gone awry or ended. The most-referred to reason for divorce in the United States is lack of communication. This implies that the two spouses do not grow together but apart. The consequences extend to the children, the extended families on both sides, mutual friends, perhaps work associates, and members of the church community. Most of all they affect the two spouses. Others may have feelings about the marriage, but the ultimate judgment belongs to the spouses.

Forgiveness and reconciliation are needed in all these relationships. But forgiveness might not start with the spouses themselves. It might start with the rest of us because we are part of the relationship. We offer support so that the people can put their lives back together. We cannot cut people out of our care, even if we blame one person rather than the other. It is not a question of who is right, it is a question of two people (or more if there are children) who are struggling to find themselves. We offer our desire for them to have an authentic life with integrity. The first step might be a reconciliation that is tolerant of the differences, and perhaps that is all the further we can go, but we know that a reconciliation of persons is the goal. Taking sides, holding grudges, continuing the division only does harm to everyone.

Jesus came to heal the sick, not the healthy. In our ecclesial communities, divorced or separated Christians can feel alienated from the community. No one needs to tell the divorced persons how difficult it is to begin again; they know it. To shun people when they are most in need is not discipleship. To shun another disciple who is hurting is to break the bond of community love. Our church community will be tested by how much we love and include those who are hurting. We are not communities of the saved, but a community of disciples "on the way," not having arrived at the end of our journey. While our ideals are firm, we might question whether or not we have taught people how to pick themselves up after a failure. Or do we teach the ideal, and when it is not reached, somehow indicate that breakages are people's chosen destiny, thereby leaving them to themselves? Sometimes judgment is an easier way to deal with others than helping.

In our parishes, groups that help the divorced Christian are living acts of reconciliation by the Church to the people, and by the people to the Church. Groups such as these do not pass judgment on others but accept people where they are, encouraging them to find God in the circumstances of their lives.

LIBERTY

More people were killed around Pietermaritzburg, South Africa, in 1989 than in Beirut or Northern Ireland. When a young black man from one of the townships was asked about the causes of the killings, he replied, "There are three reasons: politics, crime, and revenge." When asked what could be done about it he said, "The politics can be resolved, the criminal element sorted out, but revenge goes on forever."

Without the willingness to stop the downward spiral of violence that revenge feeds off of, the human race cannot extricate itself from what can only be a growing climate of revenge and violence. Throughout our world today, countries are torn apart and hatred is turned to revenge: Northern Ireland, Israel, Iran, Sri Lanka, Afghanistan, India, Uganda, Nicaragua, to mention only a few that we read about daily in the news. We do not have to go outside of our country, our cities, our neighborhoods, our families to find revenge unquenched and looking for an opportunity to break out again. Most homicides in the United States occur within the family. At some point, someone must blink. Someone must forgive without asking for recompense, for a pound of flesh or balanced scales of justice. Mercy must temper justice. Forgiveness as an act of reconciling love is the only way to break that vicious spiral. The Christian is called to live a life of love that extends to all areas and avenues of human relationships. Because the stakes are so high in a global world and the hurts so large and longstanding, forgiveness is an important Christian witness to discipleship.

Listening to one another is the necessary first step in the process of reconciliation and forgiveness. Unless we can provide models of reconciliation that show a working towards the ideal, there is no hope. A university can be that model, as can a church, a parish, a family. At a university where students come from different backgrounds, cultures, educational levels, expectations, races, creeds, and countries, a possible model for reconciliation among diverse people is concretely possible. Alumni, parents, diocese, business people, government, and benefactors can support this hope. It cannot be done by faculty, administration, or students alone, but through the community of all those who wish to participate in a grand microcosm of the world in the making. This is a model of community to be sought after. It can be an example to others that reconciliation and living together is possible. Antagonism can be suppressed in favor of listening to others. We do not wish to be a country that devolves into a practicing apartheid (apartness). To resist division is to dig in the heels of love, to build community is to walk with another.

We know that we are sinners. We cannot cast stones upon others. Yet we seek integrity, honesty, compassion, justice, and love. Where do I draw the line of minimal consideration? Divorce is one area but there are others. My own memories harbor people that I may not be able to forgive. To sit back and reflect on my history, the moments and people that have hurt me, is the first step to the healing of memories. Incest, sexual abuse, manipulation by parents, enforced dependency, and other areas are all places of hurting in people's life. We need healing. People who feel their parents did not love them, who could never show their emotions, who could only fear their parents, need a healing of memories.

In affairs of government, events that look bleak for the politician receive a "spin" so that the best, most favorable interpretation is insisted upon as the truth. "Double-speak" implies that a person can tell an untruth but really mean the truth (sophistry at its impenetrable best!). We "hold steady courses" in the face of human outcry. Rarely do we hear an acknowledgement that suffering has been put on people's backs, that burdens have been carried by the poor, the widowed, the sick on behalf of societies or public policies. Rarely do we hear that wrongs have been committed (not just "errors in judgment"). The world, I believe, would be a better place if we made room for mistakes to be honestly seen, admitted, and used as a bridge to build a new tomorrow. Perhaps instead of hiding our societal problems in the dark, we might hold them up to the light. This attitude on everyone's part would require great humility, and would place high value on service to all as the guiding light. Forgiveness and reconciliation would become ways to move forward and stay together.

PURSUIT OF HAPPINESS

To box people in because of an event that took place is to restrict even the possibility for growth and change and the life that comes with reconciliation. To be pegged forever by one event, perhaps a mistake, is unjust. The real challenge is not to box people in, but to allow for change; to exercise responsibility, to regain trust, to love again, these are the great opportunities for human growth. Yet there is something in us that likes the security of boxes, whether in the form of psychology (such as neurotics), sociology (such as misfits), politics (such as communists), anthropology (such as primitives), philosophy (such as rationalists), or theology (such as fundamentalists). Labels can damage people and we can use them to do so. Boxes make life manageable but they do damage. Breaking open a box of people might be the beginning of a new appreciation of other people and ourselves. As disciples we are called to see persons from God's perspective, not simply our own or society's perspective.

Reconciliation says that we are happier as a people together. "A person is a person through people," as Africans say so well. We recognize that we are fallible, that relationships break apart, that our best intentions go sour. Nevertheless we continue to seek contact, communication, and mutual exchange. The moment we deny our related selves, deny that there is a need for reconciliation, we become the walking dead.

The challenge of reconciliation often stems from our very selves. Happiness comes from integrity, within ourselves and nourished in others. It is very interesting that Jesus tells us to love others as we love ourselves. Over and over again, university students tell me how hard they find it to love themselves. We seem to punish and put down ourselves. The challenge to love ourselves as children of God, unique, lovable, loving, cared for, caring. Too many people think too little of themselves. That they could really be loved and lovable is beyond admission, yet they deeply want it to be true.

For the United States population, love of one's self seems automatically egotistical. That is not true. Self-love is self knowledge, and it comes from others. It is not egotistical to stand in front of a mirror, look hard and long at the image there, and say "I am a good person. I am loveable." The moment is embarrassing and makes us self-conscious. Nonetheless, the act is very Christlike: he held up a mirror to our "sinful," "outcast" selves and proved us wrong. We are loved children of God who have the freedom, joy, and privilege to play, dance, and enjoy this love. The face in the mirror is nothing less than the reflection of God.

Our pursuit of happiness is related to our understanding of ourselves. Through the events of our lives, the people we meet and fall into friendships with, and those special relationships of affective love, we find ourselves loving and lovable. To see ourselves as loving and lovable is an act of humility that allows reconciliation with others to take place.

It is interesting that the great mystic Teresa of Avila, when describing the interior castle of the human person, said that no progress from room to room in "her Father's mansion" was possible without humility. To see ourselves as God sees us is an empowerment to see others in their uniqueness. Humility makes reconciliation possible. "Learn from me," Jesus said, "for I am meek and humble of heart." In the last analysis, we are all human persons tied with other human persons at a particular time and place on this planet. We will either allow love to grow or snuff it out.

In summary, mistakes occur in the course of every human relationship. Encasing someone in psychological concrete when they make a mistake is denying the human. Disciples are not called to judge people but to empower them, seeking good in even the sinner. We are called to show tremendous virtue, by reaching out in such a way that the other person can become responsible for his or her actions, pick up the pieces and restore meaning to life. Divorce is one instance which touches everyone, requiring the Church's reconciliation. To box people into their mistakes in any form is to deny their repentance. We must draw a line somewhere and the destructiveness of revenge is a good place to start. Are there people we won't forgive? Any reconciliation challenges the individual disciple to see where she or he stands before the Lord. Can disciples accept their own relationship of love with God and make this the rock foundation of their relationship with others? Perhaps we jump too easily to others without acknowledging the love that is within us. In the end, growth in love of God is what the disciple lives and promotes—even when setbacks occur.

Further Considerations

1. Personally: Where do I most need reconciliation within myself? What events in my life still need healing? Who has shown me an example of forgiveness?

2. United States Context: What areas are most in need of reconciliation and forgiveness in the United States? Which events are signs of reconciliation and forgiveness?

3. Global Context: Where is our world most in need of reconciliation and forgiveness? Are there any examples of global forgiveness and reconciliation?

4. Church Context: What areas of Church are most in need of reconciliation and forgiveness? Which events show the act of reconciliation and forgiveness working? Do we have any outstanding examples?

Theme 7

DISCIPLESHIP: WHO WE BECOME AND HOW WE ACT

That Christians admit their need for forgiveness and reconciliation (theme 6) indicates that they care about the greater command to love God and neighbor. For example, one does not ask forgiveness of mother or father if one does not consider the relationship with one's parents important. The theme of discipleship provides the context wherein forgiveness and reconciliation have a purpose. And, as we have been developing throughout this book, discipleship gives direction and expression to the entire Christian life.

Going to school is a common experience for every American. It is not so in other countries. From the beginning of our nation, United States democracy insisted on the education of its young people in order for them to participate in our culture and exercise the freedoms that we protect. For twelve (high school), sixteen (college), or even twenty years (doctoral or professional training), we are students. Returning to take refresher courses, keeping certifications of many kinds, or returning later in life to gain more expertise, adds on more years of schooling. With all this experience of school, we know what being a student requires.

We do not use the word "disciple" often when referring to a student but that is what a student is. A master's degree in any subject signifies that one has reached a competency to teach—one has become a master who can take in students. An "apprentice" is one who puts himself or herself at the disposal of a master in order to learn. Jesus was referred to as a teacher, a rabbi, a master, even though he had no formal training. The people who gathered closely around him found their role best described as "disciple" or "student." Jesus taught them about God, with the authority and wisdom that belonged to one of his time who was a master, a teacher. To follow his teaching was to live a life in the manner of Jesus. Followers were called disciples. Discipleship describes both who we are and how we act in the imitation of Jesus Christ. Today we continue as students who listen to God's ways and respond in the same manner as Jesus.

Let us now turn to Scripture as our source for describing the journey of a disciple. We need to remember that the pattern of Jesus' own life is the totality of discipleship. Nevertheless, Scripture does single out some specific characteristics for following him, and offers some role models, such as the apostles.

Discipleship in Scripture

Let us begin with the word "disciple" itself. The term disciple (Greek *mathetes*) occurs about 250 times in the New Testament. It means one who puts themself in the school of a teacher and shares his or her views. In later Judaism the rabbis, the teachers of the law, had disciples to whom they transmitted their doctrine. These men in turn could hope to become rabbis. Jesus made no pretense of being a rabbi, although he was seen to function in that capacity. Several unique characteristics of Jesus' discipleship, as distinguished from Judaism, were that no one superseded Jesus; disciples did not strive for status as pupils, ordination was not the goal of their education, and discipleship was not something temporary. Not the law but the person of Jesus was the crucial point of reference that bound the disciple, even more closely than ties to father and mother (Matt 10:37; Luke 14:25).

Discipleship is best understood in its function as special service in the proclamation of the kingdom of God (Mark 1:17, Luke 9:60). The disciples share in this ministry of Jesus and adopt his manner of life. The identity of participating in the kingdom was seen, indeed reflected, through the pattern of Jesus' own life, death, and resurrection.[1] The evangelists agree that the center of discipleship is given by Jesus, who says that to be one of his disciples, one

[1] *The Interpreter's Dictionary*, supp., 233.

"must deny his very self, take up his cross, and follow in my steps" (Mark 8:34; Matt 10:38; Luke 14:26; John 12:25).

The New Testament restricts the notion of disciple to those who have acknowledged Jesus as their master. In the Gospels the Twelve are from the first so designated (Matt 10:1; 12:1). Beyond this intimate circle are the seventy-two who are sent on mission (Luke 10:1). These disciples were undoubtedly numerous and many gave up (John 6:66). By chapter six of the Book of Acts, "disciple" includes every believer, whether or not they had known Jesus during his early life (Acts 6:1 ff.; 9:10-26), thereby likening the faithful to the Twelve themselves (John 2:11; 8:31; 20:29).[2] Finally the word disciple becomes an ecclesiological term to describe the Church itself.

The earliest followers seemed to find in discipleship their primary identity. They called themselves "followers of the way" which is Jesus' life. However, as the message moved to Antioch and the Gentile territories, the word for follower, "Christian," took hold. We have been called Christians ever since. Nevertheless, the root of our designation as Christian remains firmly planted in the concept of discipleship.

Some of the characteristics of discipleship can be gathered into three headings: calling, personal attachment to Christ, and destiny and dignity. Intellectual and moral aptitudes are not determinative; what matters is the call, the initiative which comes from Jesus and behind him the Father who gives Jesus his disciples (John 6:39; 10:29; 17:6, 12). There is no elite group, therefore, that merits God's invitation. It is gift. Personal attachment to Christ is "to follow," and expresses the necessary attachment to the person of Jesus. One conforms his or her life to that of the savior (Mark 8;34; 10:21: John 12:26). Destiny and dignity means that the disciple is called to share the very destiny of the master: to carry his cross (Mark 8:34), to drink his cup (Mark 10:38), and finally to receive from him the kingdom (Matt 19:28). From this time on, even to give a glass of water will not lose its reward (Matt 10:42). Thus the relationship to Jesus brings the model of Jesus' love to bear our lives. We are followers of Jesus and live in the same commitment to God.

[2]Leon-Dufour, *Dictionary of Biblical Theology*, 125.

The education of the disciples is central to the Gospels, indicating that discipleship is a process brought about by continual exposure to Jesus. In Mark, Jesus chooses his disciples, brings them with him before the authorities, to his family, lets them see his healing power, and explains to them the parables. They lack understanding of discipleship because they do not yet see the whole of Jesus' life, which will culminate in his death and resurrection. Until then, their knowledge will be partial. They do have faith as professed by Peter, but also carry Peter's misunderstanding that Jesus need not suffer, and the ambition of James and John as to who will be first. Sometimes they are a foil for Jesus, other times his intimate companions. They receive special instructions and are told about his death and resurrection. Still, at the death, they run away in fear. Whereas Matthew generally understands the use of the word disciple to mean the twelve apostles, Luke differentiates between the Twelve and the rest of the disciples (6:13; Acts 6:2). This differentiation seems to indicate the special structure of ministry: first the Twelve and then those who are commissioned. "Disciple," however, designates the vocation of every Christian who is commissioned to preach the gospel; it is not limited to the Twelve. For this reason, the Sermon on the Mount in Matthew becomes the Sermon on the Plain in Luke, addressed to the seventy-two as well.

In John, discipleship is identical with being a Christian, with believing, abiding in the word, practicing brotherly and sisterly love. Disciple stresses John's vertical relationship of humanity to divinity, or of us to the Son, and hence the Father. A disciple is a person whom we encounter and follow. In the last discourse, the washing of the feet, the beautiful image of our connectedness to God as vine to branch, followed by the Eucharistic Meal, emphasize the personal relationship to God. It is God himself whom they hear and thus all become "disciples of God" (John 6:45).[3]

A wide variety of examples of discipleship exists throughout the Gospels and teaches us how to act. Peter is the most frequently mentioned apostle, Mary the mother of Jesus is specially developed in the infancy narratives, and John as the Beloved Disciple knows Jesus' affection. Beyond these central persons, another whole range

[3]Ibid., 233.

of examples appears and we catch glimpses in memorable people such as Matthew, Philip, Thomas, Bartholomew, Zaccheus, the Samaritan Woman, the Gerasene demoniac, Martha and Mary, Mary Magdalene, Bartimeus, and Nicodemus. We also hear how to be a disciple in stories, for example the widow's mite, the rich man and Lazarus, the shepherd who lost one of his hundred sheep, and the good Samaritan. Over and over, throughout the Gospels, discipleship is presented, turned to a slightly different angle, given further explanation, and unfolded in the light of the encounter with Jesus. In a word, discipleship is the lesson of each Gospel.

Let us pull together the various scriptural presentations into a systematic whole.

The Triad: God, Jesus, Us.

From the perspective of God, discipleship is an invitation to participate in co-creating a world of goodness and love. The project of salvation is done in this world by human beings in cooperation with God's graciousness, working in a creative transformation of the world. God has left open to the human family a significant role in salvation. It is as if God says, "Here, learn what I am all about." In this way we are created in the image of God and also act in the image of God. We too love, forgive, are compassionate, and pursue justice as God does. In these activities, God has wonderfully committed his grace: when we love, God is there. When we have compassion—God is there. When we become reconciled to one another—God is there. When we strive to become the best we can be even in the face of adversity, uncertainty, and struggle—God is there. It is as if God is woven into the fabric of humanity through these moments. In these acts we experience God most clearly; they are windows into the mystery of a God who is for us.

From the perspective of Jesus, he was more than a disciple to the Father, he was the obedient son. We are invited by God through Jesus to share in the same relationship but, of course, in a slightly different way because we are not Jesus. We say with Paul that we "put on the mind of Christ," that with the evangelists we "follow Jesus in discipleship," and with our tradition through people like Thomas 'a Kempis we "imitate Christ." We never become "other Christs," but we follow Jesus analogously, through similarity-in-difference. Jesus was uniquely son of the Father. We are children of God "by adoption," "born out of time," above all "by faith." To be a mirror image of Jesus would never save us. To love as Jesus did, completely, compassionately, and unconditionally, is what will save us.

Because we are not Jesus, the question, "What would Jesus do if he were here?" can be met with cynicism, saying that this is pure escapism because we never know. But the truth contained in this question is good and practically helpful for Christian disciples. The question brings our own best aspirations, hopes, honesty, faith, and courage to the arena of our relationship with Jesus, and asks us to transcend our pettiness and to think and judge in light of those values of Jesus that guide our lives. This is a profound sentiment and a transforming activity that is placed ultimately before God.

From the perspective of us, discipleship is a way of life that commands our allegiance, shapes the choices that follow, opens a way of service, and a life in love into which we enter. A disciple is honored to be invited, acknowledges his or her dependence upon the master, and spreads the good news to others. Disciples know that they are not alone, that a family of disciples surrounds them, that the power of their own discipleship is supported and empowered by God's presence within the group. Disciples rely on one another to discern where God is in the world, where the Master is calling them to go, and how they are to proceed. The most immediate group of disciples is the local church, then the entire Church.

Disciples know that they do not have the final word but that they do have the final commitment to make. It is an all or nothing proposition; no one can be "partially a disciple," one either is or is not. True, we all know that we can be more generous and loving, that we are sinners, that we could better disciples at times, but we acknowledge that we are imperfect disciples "on the way." This is a description of every human person.

Retrieving Discipleship for Today

Passing information on to others is part of the generativity of humanity. Discipleship in the sense of learning exists in all cultures and is necessary in order for any tradition to be passed down. For example, among Native Americans, the concept of discipleship is strong. It is a way of communicating the wisdom from one group to another, including the origins and ethics of the tribe. This is often done by one person who is called a "grandfather," although not by blood, rather as a teacher. A "grandson" learns the secrets from the grandfather. Doled out in small amounts, this knowledge is power. Secrecy and mystery are important, as are the rites by which a grandson proves ready to hear the knowledge.

The grandson hears in the rite that one cannot obtain wisdom without suffering, that it is never given cheaply, and that it cannot be held carelessly. In a strong sense, the people of the tribe are themselves being passed down through this information. It is survival, gift, wisdom, and identity. To destroy this information is to destroy the people's stories and their cherished knowledge of who they are. Collective amnesia means to be lost in the world.

There are many ways of passing down information. For a Zen student, it requires many hours a day strictly obeying a Zen master. For an apprentice, it requires performing the actions of the master little by little. A medicine man will apprentice a younger man and gradually pass knowledge down. Usually strict discipline like fasting, obedience, or a trial is required to make one ready to receive this information. The sacredness is thereby reinforced. Hence, wisdom is always special and not to be identified with everyday kinds of knowledge.

In the Christian life, no one is born a disciple; we become disciples. The test is faith which goes beyond blood, and a knowledge of God that reflects wisdom and not human philosophy. While a special knowledge called the Gnostic tradition was connected to the Christian discipleship, it was rejected. Christian discipleship is not exclusive, secret, or other-worldly. It requires the free choice to live one's life in love and love one's life in God and others. It belongs to every believer.

The metaphor of discipleship does not stand alone in the gospel but is complemented by a closeness to Jesus that can only be described by the image of familial blood. When Jesus returns to his home town of Nazareth, some people tell him that his mother and brothers are looking for him. He gazes around at those seated in the circle and continues: "These are my mother and my brothers. Whoever does the will of God is brother and sister and mother to me" (Mark 3:33). Disciples are not only followers but family: they belong to Jesus, to one another, and share in the joy and blessings that accrue to an entire household. This totality always is much more than any individual can expect or use. In our relationship to Jesus, we also become brothers and sisters and mothers and fathers to each other.

To follow along with this interconnection, people ask why we call a priest "Father." Simply put, it is because of this familial faith reality. The presider at worship is responsible for the nourishment of the people in liturgy and the sacraments on behalf of the people. It is with affection that we recognize our faith relationship. The other side of the coin is that we call the presider to be nourisher on behalf of us; we call others to ministry. This call to ministry extends to men and women religious who are called "brother" and "sister." In many places within the Christian Church, lay people who take on ministries are referred to as brother or sister. In the Philippines, for example, the leading woman in the barrio is married yet referred to with respect as "sister." Our words for another are longstanding in our tradition; they can be changed, but their importance is clear: we are family to each other. Our language reflects this truth. We wish now to specify discipleship in its American context. Although this task is never-ending, open to new experiences, and judged by its effects, nevertheless discipleship seeks the particularization of context.

Life, Liberty, and the Pursuit of Happiness

LIFE

Discipleship means to love God above all things and your neighbor as yourself, as the Jesus Event shows us. We then enter upon a lifetime journey. The gospel centers us and lures us onwards. We find that this same Spirit of Jesus and the Father unites us into fellowship with others. To stay centered upon Christ is the challenge of the Church and each individual.

When God invites us to love more, or to love in new ways, or to love again, we are in the process of conversion. I remember in math classes we "converted" dollars to cents, decimals to percentages, quarts to liters, yards to meters. Our conversion process as human persons is similar, in that we become other than what we are. The difference in faith is that we become the same "other" all the time: that is, more loving persons. If all conversion charts went from dollars to love, decimals to love, quarts to love, yards to love, then we would grasp Christian conversion.

Disciples undergo conversion all day long. To everything that we touch, every event we enter into, every person we meet, we bring our love. The interchange between ourselves and others depends partially upon us and love does enter in. One could rightly say that we are in a constant act of converting all to love, including ourselves in the process. Simple and small ways present themselves to us every day: a cup of coffee with a friend who is down, a word of gratitude that is unnecessary, a gesture of tenderness, a kind word.

Along with small conversions, we have larger and more decisive ones. They usually take the form of life decisions. They may require taking responsibility for our actions, or following through on our commitments, or taking the initiative for situations in our lives, or making new commitments. As all freedoms, conversion demands a freedom FROM in order to be free FOR life in discipleship. These moments are critical because they pry open our deepest recesses.

Oftentimes these conversions are as quiet and personal as they are forceful and deep. When one is in love, the great conversion is trust. Trust, like a blade of grass, does not make much noise, is hardly noticed, and does not seem to require much attention. Nevertheless, to trust God or another more and more requires the deepest and most forceful letting go of self. This quiet and personal trust renders us most vulnerable as human persons to others; we can be wounded deepest, and be scarred for life. Yet love will have it no other way. As disciples we accept the risks because the prize is so precious. To lose control of life and hand that control to love is easier said than done. Yet it is the way of discipleship.

Conversions are both personal and communal. We call ourselves to conversion because we see God's Spirit working in our midst. Through the community we find God. For example, we may not know what is happening to people down the block in our parish, in another part of our city, in rural areas, in other cities and regions, and throughout the world. When the bishops write a letter concerning evangelization, we all are called to hear the Spirit speaking among them. When the bishops write a letter on peace, or on economic justice, we all are called to hear the Spirit there. Because something is not within my immediate experience, I do not discard it as untrue. The heightening of my consciousness is a call to conversion. I choose to take on these realities because I trust other people's expression of the pain and suffering they undergo. What I can do about this pain remains to be seen.

One example of how we have called ourselves to conversion, though not totally, is in the "women's issues." Women in the culture and Church have called attention to the language used, the roles prescribed for them, the bias in pay, the power structures, and countless areas of unconscious victimization. The call to conversion comes from others and clearly challenges us to a change of living because the status quo damages the love Jesus showed us. The conversion is not to accept "women's issues" but to recognize that both women and men must change. These are not "women's issues" but human issues involving women and men.

Another example is the "social justice issues." We did not hear this phrase years ago, but we have come to see that structures are oppressing people and we help maintain those structures. Having been called to see people's plight and hear their cries, we realize that a conversion is needed. Others, particularly the poor themselves, have heightened our consciousness. It is up to us to accept the needed conversion in our lives. Discipleship does not break people into groups, factions, or policies; it seeks love of neighbor. Where dehumanization takes place, whether systemically in structures or in individuals, love resists it. We may not know which strategy is the best for humanization—there is more than one right answer—but we can all agree on what will not be acceptable because it dehumanizes.

LIBERTY

God never forces us to love. God never forces us to change. God invites us in our freedom to love and to change. Only we can do it. Nevertheless, when we desire something good, like being loved and loving others, then we are willing to pay the purchase price demanded for it. It is far easier to exercise our freedom within a love relationship than outside it. Love provides freedom with its identity. Like a bee looking for honey, so is freedom looking for love. Freedom does not provide its own end, it serves the human person. What and whom one chooses depends upon what one wants in life. Love of God and neighbor is the goal that freedom now serves. Conversion calls upon freedom to live faithfully towards greater love in all its choices.

The choices before us are the concrete ways we activate discipleship. People need goals. The disciple's main goal gathers in all others as subordinate and thus life has an integrity, a wholeness, and a coherency to it. As Augustine insightfully expressed it, "Love and do what you will." Love sums up and infiltrates everything that we do. To love fully is to choose well.

Many goals are provided in our culture. Goals of success, money, possessions, and fame swirl around us. People sacrifice everything to attain these goals. A survey of athletes asked whether they would take a drug that would harm them if they could break a world record, and most said "yes." The drive in us is strong. We wish to be different, leave a mark, be in lights for once, make the evening news. But is that worth any sacrifice? "What does it profit a man to gain the world and suffer the loss of his soul?" Disciples know the goal that brings happiness and is within the grasp of any human person, and that is to live this discipleship of love.

In an atmosphere of love, conversion and change are more easily called forth. A loving family, a loving community, love of a friend ground us, acknowledge that we are in this together, helps us support one another. Through love we realize that the other person is important and will not walk away.

To be a loving support to others in community, family, friendship is an act of love that allows conversion to take place. Without that support, fear of rejection often stops any change at all. Codependency often keeps another from changing, and then fear substitutes for love. My grandmother gave me the sage advice that, "A man convinced against his will is of the same opinion still." I remember her repeating that many times. To me it means that people change themselves. Force never works; love does.

Pursuit of Happiness

The pursuit of happiness requires continual conversion. Pursuit indicates the journey that leads the way, not the end being grasped. We do whatever is necessary to love as Jesus has taught us. To understand the love of Jesus, and to keep it before us as our goal, is necessary. Hence we must come to know Jesus, not only as individuals but also in the community. The word "discern" is used a great deal today, and sometimes is overused; nevertheless, it expresses the key concept around which conversion turns. To discern God's presence in ourselves, in events, in structures, in the rhythm of the ups and downs of life is the necessary requirement before we know how and where to convert all to love.

We begin in ourselves and return from activity back to our reflective selves. Every disciple builds a core of values and habits that we call a spirituality. Building this core in relationship to Jesus is our task. It would be correct to say that the spirituality of discipleship is the theme of this book.

Prayer brings us in contact with our core values. We come to know Jesus by prayer, both personal and communal. We learn of Jesus by breaking open the scriptures, especially the Gospels, in personal reading, bible study courses, and sermons. We also learn of Jesus by living and reflecting upon the patterns of God's dealing with us. Time to reflect is necessary. Sometimes another person to reflect with is helpful—a prayer partner, a spiritual director, a group, a prayer director.

A retreat, whether a day, several days, a week, or more, is another example. Retreats are marvelous "classrooms" of learning, in a non-traditional sense of classroom. The hustle and bustle of our everyday world can be "tuned down" in order to "tune up" deeper feelings and desires that cannot come to the surface so easily. "Noise" in all its forms distorts hearing. We all have noise interfering with our contact with the spiritual dimension. A habit of prayer grounds us in our relationship with Jesus and others. Praying with the family, husband, wife, children, a fiancee, friends, the sick, all of these help build our communal core in Christ.

Spiritual directors also help us come into contact with Jesus and often help us find patterns in our lives. They also help us interpret feelings and desires that we might otherwise downplay or neglect. People have spiritual directors for short periods or sometimes for years.

To walk in Jesus' footprints we must know him. To know when and where to turn on our journey through life, we need to be able to recognize his footprints going down other roads; then we follow.

In summary, conversion means to bring everything and everyone in our lives within the grasp of greater and deeper love. Our conversions are mostly small and daily, but can also be large and decisive. They are personal and also communal. We have examples of communal conversions that raise our consciousness and sensitize us so that we accept the suffering of others as our own. Love seeks the good of all, not a few. Our freedom serves love, and love provides freedom with its goal. Change occurs best in a loving atmosphere. The challenge, then, is to know God in Jesus and to discern his invitations to us. Many personal and communal helps are available to aid us in discerning whether something is truly God's call, and then what response is needed. Conversion, in the last analysis, is the spirituality of every disciple.

Further Considerations

1. Personally: How do I most often experience my following of Christ? When do I most feel like a disciple? When don't I?

2. United States Context: What dimensions of the United States context make discipleship difficult? Which make it easy?

3. Global Context: Who are models of discipleship in our world?

4. Church Context: Where do I experience the Church as disciple? Where not? How can the Church live out discipleship in the United States today? In the world?

Theme 8

CHURCH: WHO WE ARE AND WHAT WE DO

We are Christians—together. Disciples are not different in faith; we all possess the same Spirit of Jesus and the Father. The earliest potential division among the first disciples was an argument about whether faith had distinctions: did someone have to go through the Mosaic covenant in order to become Christian? The answer was "no." Anyone with the Spirit can enter into baptism and become a disciple within the community called Church. As Vatican II reiterated, the earliest experience of the apostles was that people know and possess the Spirit outside the Church community. This is well and good. The Christian experience is that this Spirit gathers, unites, consolidates, intertwines, and involves people with God and one another. No apostle sat down under a fig tree and thought, "Wouldn't it be nice to have a Church?" On the contrary, Church happened because the Spirit gathered people together. This is God's doing, not humanity's. The result is a humanity as brother and sister under the same God; we have a growing familial relationship with one another because of our God.

The Church is a divine institution with a human face. The Church itself is a testimony to its founding event: the incarnation. As such, the Church is a sacrament of God's encounter with humanity.

A common image of Church is the large, steepled building usually located on a street corner. Our common usage of the word Church describes who we are as a people: Catholic Church, Baptist Church, Methodist Church, Lutheran Church. I was surprised to see students refer to Judaism at the time of Jesus as "the Jewish

143

Church," while recognizing that Jews worshipped in synagogues, but on second thought I could see their rationale. "Church" has become a designation of religious people. No doubt anyone can slip into the image that Jesus worshipped in a church building and held his last supper in one, and that the disciples went out and built church buildings based upon the same architectural plan Monsignor Jones uses. It is just as easy to slip into the language fallacy that Jesus called his followers "church." What was Jesus' understanding of who we are together?

This last topic extends the theme of discipleship to a community of disciples. It completes the necessary themes that we need for an adequate Christology. Let us begin with an understanding of Church from the first century, then apply it today.

The Church in Scripture

The etymology of the word itself (English "church," Scottish *kirk*, German *Kirche*, Dutch *kerk*) is derived from the late Greek work *kyriakon* which means "the Lord's (house)." The Greek word *ekklesia* signified the assembly of the citizens of a city for legislative or deliberative purposes. It included only the citizens who enjoyed full rights, and thus the word implies both the dignity of the members and the legality of the assembly. The Greek word had no religious usage. It was adopted by the Septuagint, or Greek translation of the Old Testament, to render the Hebrew word *kahal* which means "the religious assembly." It became used, in Christianity, to designate the local community of believers who assembled in the name of, and at the invitation of, the Lord.[1] Thus the word Church means "those who have assembled and will continue to assemble in the name of the Lord."

Although the Old Testament has no special word for this intimate and real contact with God and one another, the New Testament uses the descriptive word, *koinonia*, which expresses communion with God and one another. The desire to be in communion with God is the basis of every religion. Christianity attests that in Jesus this desire for communion is realized. God abides with us and we with God.

[1] Mckenzie, *Dictionary of the Bible,* 133.

Love of God and neighbor come together in a visible community, where love of one another (fraternal union) is the hallmark of love of God. "One heart and one soul" (Acts 4:32) distinguishes these first Christian communities. The sign of their unity is seen and realized in the breaking of the bread (the sacrament of the Eucharist). In the Jerusalem community, the unity went further to the sharing of goods, and in the Gentile communities, Paul took up a collection to help needy communities (2 Cor 8–9). Suffering persecution together also contributed to this unity of hearts (2 Cor 1:7).

For Paul, the believer is attached to Christ by faith and baptism. By their own sufferings and death Christians are made like Christ in his passion, death, and resurrection (2 Cor 4:14; Rom 8:17). Sharing in the Eucharistic Body of Christ brings about both communion with the Son and union of members. The Holy Spirit sets the seal on the intimate communion between believers (2 Cor 13:13; Phil 2:1).

For John, the disciple who welcomes the "Word of Life" enters into communion with its witnesses (apostles) and through them with Jesus and the Father (1 John 1; 3; 2:24). Christians "abide" in the love of the Father and the Son (John 14:20; 15:4, 7). The authentic sign of this communion is the observation of Jesus' commandments. The essential nourishment is the power of the Holy Spirit and the Eucharistic bread (John 14:17; 5:56).[2]

The Greek word *ekklesia* was used to designate a particular communal reality. It is by no means the dominating or central term. Of the 112 appearances of *ekklesia* in the New Testament, ninety percent are found in Paul's letters, Acts, and Revelation. The word *ekklesia* appears only twice in the Synoptic Gospels: in Matthew 16:18 and 18:18. The teachings of Jesus are stated in terms of the kingdom of God. But the foundations of Church are clear in the Synoptic Gospels, especially in the formation of the disciples and other followers of Jesus. Jesus demanded personal attachment to himself, and the disciples received mission from him. In Matthew, *ekklesia* is clearly identified with this group which Jesus himself formed and which he commanded be continued by his disciples after his departure.

[2]Leon-Dufour, *Dictionary of Biblical Theology,* 86.

I do not think that it is possible to read the Gospels without acknowledging the strong invitation to discipleship and model given in Jesus' life. Discipleship is so pervasive that it might go unarticulated and taken for granted. I think it is reasonably clear that the Gospels were written with the intention of teaching others how to follow Jesus. Discipleship is the purpose of the Gospels.

In Acts, *ekklesia,* used twenty-three times, means the local church, usually the local church at Jerusalem that sent out missionaries and expanded. The other local churches were extensions of the Jerusalem church.

Paul uses *ekklesia* sixty-five times and for the first time in the plural, which implies the equality of the separate local churches. In Ephesians and Colossians the word is used to refer to the entire worldwide assembly of the followers of Jesus, which is conceived as one great assembly, formulated in Paul's famous image of the Church compared to a body, with Christ as its head (Eph 1:22-23; 1 Cor 12:12 ff.). The model of love based upon how husbands treat their wives (Eph 5:22-32) was suggested in the Synoptics with Jesus as the bridegroom (Matt 9:15; Mark 2:19; Luke 5:34), which harks back to the older image of Yahweh as the spouse of Israel. For Paul the local churches are united into a single organization which is called the Church. Theology has called this union the mystical body. Its life is drawn from the enduring presence of Jesus through the Spirit. It is of divine origin with a human face.

The reality of Church is so rich that more than one hundred cognate expressions may be distinguished to express the idea of Church, but some scholars group them into ten general categories. Let us examine them briefly.

1) The saints and the sanctified. Here *ekklesia* is viewed from the standpoint of God's action toward humanity. In this case *ekklesia* becomes equivalent to those whom God has chosen, gathered, foreknown, justified, glorified, sanctified (1 Cor 1:2). The saints are those who have received the Holy Spirit by rebirth in baptism and depend upon the activity of the Father (Luke 11:13, John 10:36), the Son, and Spirit in relation to the community (John 10:36; 17:15-20).

2) Believers and faithful. *Ekklesia* may be viewed from the standpoint of communal response to God's action through Christ, a response which is empowered by the Holy Spirit. Christ calls people

to follow him—to be his disciples, to be with him, to be sent by him. Those who respond constitute *ekklesia.* Over seventy-five passages in the New Testament support the idea of the Church as the community of believers.

3) Slaves and servants. *Ekklesia* may be viewed from the basic duties which this response of faith entails. The Church is comprised of those who through faith have accepted duties of slaves, servants, stewards, ministers, witnesses, confessors, ambassadors, soldiers, and friends. As slaves to Christ, they are committed to goodness, and live under his power. This is the opposite of the slavery of fear, to the law, the flesh, the world, and Satan. Slaves of Christ are free in relation to the flesh. To be a slave of Christ is to imitate his humiliation, lowliness, suffering (Matt 10:24, Mark 10:44-45; John 13:16). To be a slave is to be a witness, an apostle, who proclaims Jesus' gospel. All believers are ipso facto servants *(diakonia),* and the same Spirit energizes all forms of service. Many forms of service are possible.

4) The people of God. The Christian *ekklesia* is viewed through the New Testament as the people of God and therefore a continuation and consummation of the Old Testament covenant community. A recognition of solidarity with Israel is present throughout the New Testament. The use of the term people of God seems not specific enough to encompass the reality of disciple.[3]

5) Kingdom and temple. The Church as the gathering of God's people is viewed in terms of those institutions which had long been central in the life of Israel—the kingdom and the temple. The Church is never identified with the kingdom of God. The temple, in fact, made Jerusalem the holy city, something the Samaritans resented. Early Christians continued the temple image as the place where God touched earth, but transferred the physical place to the individual believers gathered together in the Spirit. Jesus' presence was decisive as this new temple between God and humankind. Jesus was seen to be the cornerstone and foundation for the living stones wherein the presence of God dwelt in his Holy Spirit. Within this temple, Jesus is the High Priest uniting God and humankind. His perfect obedience signified his closeness to God's will and his per-

[3]The Interpreter's Dictionary, 610.

son sacrificed for God's revelation made him the channel of eternal salvation to all who obey him.[4]

6) Household and family. The Church is understood to be the eschatological gathering of God's people into his household, to become his house (*oikos* means the house and we derive the word ecumenical to mean the movement of gathering Christians within the same house). House and household are synonymous with "kingdom," "temple," "nation." Another familial analogy is the Church as the bride of Christ.[5]

7) The new Exodus. Many Old Testament typological comparisons are used to describe the various dimensions of the Church: Adam, Noah and the flood, the captivity by Babylon. But the most prominent is the Exodus: the sojourn, the conflict, plagues, crossing the Red Sea, the covenant, manna, the ark, Aaronic priesthood, the succession from Moses to Joshua, and the Jordan crossing. Matthew especially draws upon the parallels to the Old Testament in Moses, Israel, and Covenant on Sinai with Jesus.[6]

8) Vineyard and flock. The Church is described by a wide range of agricultural analogies, all evocative of the Church's dependence on God, of the qualitative necessity of producing fruit, and of the imminent processes of judgment. The comparison of God's people to the vineyard is familiar (Mark 12:1-12; Matt 20:1-16; 21:33-43), as is Israel to the fig tree (Matt 21:18-22; Luke 13:6-9), and the most used analogy of the Church as God's flock. Jesus is the shepherd who gives his life for the sake of the flock, who gathers the maverick members into the fold. Jesus is also symbolized as the lamb of God who takes away the sins of the world.[7]

9) One body in Christ. Paul uses the image of one body in Christ (Rom 12:5; Eph 1:23). This body binds together into a *koinonia*, or communion, of life and righteousness over which Christ rules. Christ is the head of the body.[8]

10) The new humanity. The Church is viewed as the beginning of a new creation, a new humanity, in which Jesus is the new Adam, whose image all are destined to bear.

[4]Ibid., 611.
[5]Ibid., 614.
[6]Ibid., 613.
[7]Ibid., 614.
[8]Ibid.

In summary, the Church is centered on God as revealed in Jesus the Christ. The memory of God's promise and the hope that only God can realize are essential traits which call the believer into this relationship best symbolized in the death and resurrection of Christ. The Church is knitted together by the action of the Holy Spirit, who uses gifts (charisms) to empower the Church's work and determine its duties. The Church is a new creation, a growing organism, that bears responsibility for the whole of creation. It is localized and embodied in particular temporal events, in empirical social relationships, yet points beyond these to a reality which is ontologically ultimate and eschatologically final. Thus the Church is God's chosen instrument for action in this world, the sign and channel of God's love for the world.[9]

The Triad: God, Jesus, Us

From the perspective of God, the Church signifies those who have come to believe. In the plan of salvation, belief makes us brothers and sisters to each other. Sharing the same faith, we belong simultaneously to God and others. The power of God's kingdom is made present in the person of the Holy Spirit who unites all believers. The Holy Spirit unleashes God's gifts within and through these believers called Church, the assembled and assembling in the Lord. The gifts of the sacraments, signs of God's commitment of himself to this community, continue to nourish, refresh, reconcile, and unite us; they call forth love, self-renunciation, compassion, and service. These gifts are given for the sake of all humanity and are called forth by the community in relationship to one another. The Church becomes a sign, a sacrament, of God's saving power in this world. Entrance into and empowerment of this Church come in and through belief in Jesus Christ. A community of disciples occurs.

From the perspective of Jesus, God's kingdom is the message. Those who have heard Jesus bear particular responsibility to continue in the kingdom and preach its message. These disciples who follow Jesus can depend upon the resources of the Spirit that comes through each one of their beliefs. The sum of believers is greater

[9]Ibid., 616.

and possesses more gifts of sanctification than any one part. This sum of believers depends for its life upon the Spirit who animates the whole and the individuals. The Church is a microcosm of the world, of the way the kingdom comes.

The Church is not identical with the kingdom but is a sign of that kingdom. This Church exists because of that Spirit, hence we say it is divinely founded by Jesus. It is an internal relationship with God that makes Church possible. So deeply did Karl Rahner understand this that he called all those who lived in God, and yet were not identified members of the Church, an anonymous but real part of this Church. It is the same Spirit that makes us one and this unity is of God's origin; we witness and testify to it.

From our perspective, God has given us the Church through Jesus who has called us. We need the ongoing support, nourishment, and life that the sacraments and liturgical services provide. We draw strength and courage from others who also share in this same life. We see others struggle, fail, become reconciled, and move ahead like ourselves. We see, hear, and touch the presence of God in other people and their actions. Divinely animated but with a human face, the Church remains aware of its sinfulness and its total dependence upon God. To judge is God's prerogative, we follow Jesus and live this discipleship as best we can. We share in the collective wisdom of this group, its heritage of believers for two thousand years, its tradition of belief, literature, prayer, scripture, and inculturation of faith, and all those intangibles that make up this tradition.

We know that we are the Church, that the Church is better and holier for us, and that we are holier and better for the others in this Church. We call each other to ever more faithful discipleship to the Lord. We ask ministers to help us in our needs, to be responsible for our gifts, to preserve the message, and to call us to fidelity. These ministers are our pope, bishops, priests, deacons, religious, catechists, administrators, teachers, preachers, council members, volunteers, people helping permanently and temporarily, the married and unmarried, elderly and youth, students and businesspeople, retired and unemployed. Some ministries are offices that people accept, others depend on the charisms of the individual. In both cases this Church is sponsored by the Holy Spirit. We live through and in this supportive, sustaining love.

In time, we come to love the Church in the same way people come to love their country. The Church becomes a group whose faces I have never seen, but I love them too. They extend throughout the world, are different in color, ethnicity, language, and culture—but I love them. And they love me. In this love for Church as a group, I come to also love "humanity" as a group—they are people I have never seen, different from me, but I love them too. By the love for Church I am pulled onward to love humanity. The love of God and love of neighbor continue to ring true. Love for the Church is not an end in itself, does not stop with itself, is not inward and exclusive. The dynamic of love pushes through the Church to the world, the neighbor, humanity. Again we learn that this is how God loves. We also learn, perhaps to our astonishment, that God loves humanity *through* this believing community of disciples.

Now understanding of the relation of the church to the world becomes clearer: we are indeed servants of others. We are a sacrament for others to see and hear the God who loves them. Like a nerve center that registers God's presence, we rejoice in humanity's loving God and are hurt by humanity's lack of love. In this way we are witness to others; we are a sacrament, we are servants of the Lord, we witness to the truth of God's love for us, proof that we belong to God and to one another. The truth and rightness of God's salvation becomes clear for a moment, as if we get a glimpse into the mind of God. Our place and purpose within this plan of salvation comes into focus. This is Church.

Retrieving Church for Today

The concerns of United States Catholic life can be glimpsed in the leading news stories of 1986. Forty-four American and Canadian editors ranked the leading religious stories:

1. Controversy related to restrictions on the authority of Archbishop Raymond Hunthausen of Seattle.

2. Controversy related to the revocation of Fr. Charles Curran's status as a professor of theology at the Catholic University of America.

3. Approval and publication of the United States bishops' pastoral letter, "Economic Justice for All."

4. The Church-aided, peaceful overthrow of the Marcos regime in the Philippines.

5. Church-state conflict in Nicaragua, and criticism of the United States' aid to anti-government guerrillas.

6. The interfaith prayer summit for peace at Assisi in October.

7. The letter of the Congregation for the Doctrine of Faith, "The Pastoral Care of Homosexual Persons."

8. The financial needs of elderly religious.

9. Papal travels to nine countries.

10. Church involvement in efforts to aid farmers in crisis.

The five leading newsmakers were, in order: Archbishop Raymond Hunthausen, Father Curran, Pope John Paul II, Cardinal Joseph Ratzinger, and Corazon Aquino.

These events run the gamut from national problems to international ones. Numbers one, two, three, five, eight, and ten are specifically American issues. It is instructive that the first two leading stories concern themselves with internal Church workings or "politics." While the issues are complex, those concerned have argued freedom and due process as part of the procedural problem. In each case a lack of attention to American concerns was raised. These items also indicate the focus of attention upon the internal dynamics of United States Catholic discipleship. A great deal of energy has been siphoned off into these internal conflicts—energy which in my judgment could be better spent outwardly on human rights, peace, justice, and reconciliation. No one, however, can be exempt from the need to put one's own house in order and the energy that takes. Still we need to move beyond many of these inward-gazing concerns to far more drastic and life threatening issues. It would be a great disaster for all to fiddle while Rome burns.

We must call ourselves, and listen to the call of others, to crucial issues. I believe we will overcome our own possible pettiness when we focus upon the truly devastating and complex issues. Perhaps we can come together over these issues and resolve our intellectually ideological preferences when we have to deal with doing something about important issues. Both liberals and conservatives come together and feed the hungry, no matter what their stance. Our world is in need of such action. I believe it would bring harmony, though not necessarily unity—by this I mean that people would respect one another and still hold different views—if we worked on strategic responses to pressing human issues. Militarism, sexism, ageism, racism, neo-colonialism, cultural imperialism, and economic exploitation are a few problems we can address.

It is instructive that the World Council of Churches brought very different and often bitterly opposed doctrinal churches together over the "Faith and Order" area of their concern. In other words, groups that opposed each other both agreed that missionary and charitable works had to be undertaken, and they worked side by side on them, thus creating a new avenue for communicating with each other. It is this kind of shared experience that allows us to appreciate one another and be willing to listen, no matter how different we are.

Some information that might help put United States Catholicism into perspective with the rest of the world: according to the Vatican's 1988 figures, one-sixth of the world is Catholic, approximately 879.4 million people. The *1986 Statistical Yearbook of the Catholic Church* listed the countries with the largest number of Catholics as: Brazil, 122.67 million; Mexico, 76.49 million; Italy, 56.11 million; the United States, 53.55 million; and France, 46.18 million.

As of July 26, 1988, the maximum of 120 voting cardinals had been selected. They select the pope. By composition they originate from: Europe 81 (48 percent), Latin America 24 (16 percent), Africa 18 (12 percent), Asia & Oceania 19 (13 percent; 15 from Asia, 4 from Oceania), North America 17 (11 percent) out of 159 total.

The dimensions of the Church are many and we grasp only a portion of them. The totality is never comprehended by anyone. Nor is the Holy Spirit. No one has the totality of the Spirit's guidance and no one possesses all the charisms of the Church. We need each other and the truth that each brings to the Church.

Church does not exist in the abstract but in the concrete, lived experience of people. Therefore let us look at some of the dimensions of the United States Church as challenged by the gospel of Jesus.

Life, Liberty, the Pursuit of Happiness

LIFE

The Church is life-giving. It does not exist for itself but for others. At the same time it builds up its own faith in a Church of disciples. Thus we have an internal and external thrust to the Church. The internal thrust is a celebration of the life of the Lord in our midst, and the external thrust is the mission that the Church proclaims to the entire world and through all time. For now, we will focus on the internal dimension.

The Church's purpose is the preaching of the gospel, and the Church does this through the life-giving nourishment represented in the sacraments, especially the central sacrament of the Eucharist. There, at the table of the Lord, we re-covenant ourselves by listening to the Lord's word being broken open in the community, and by receiving the Lord's nourishment and thereby becoming nourishment for others. Thus, at one and the same time, the Church celebrates its life in the Lord and commits itself to be given away. The Church, as disciple of Jesus, accepts being bread broken and wine poured out for others. This is the celebration of who we are before the Lord and one another. Love of God and love of neighbor come together at this meal.

The Eucharistic Meal is never an escape but always a greater insertion into discipleship. We bring ourselves and our world to the Lord and put them in his hands. From those same hands we receive the encouragement to trust in him more and more.

The changes in the liturgy since Vatican II have opened up the wealth of our entire worshipping history. At a later time in history, generations will look back at one of the great moments in our two thousand year tradition: the moment when we insisted on the celebration in the vernacular, or the people's own language. The importance of the liturgical changes is just beginning to reveal itself. The twenty-first century will be a time of great solidification. It takes time to develop symbols because they come from the emotions and heart of every person. They develop from the inside out, not the outside in. We have experienced a breaking of symbols in the United States and have not yet managed to develop new symbols. True symbols cannot be imposed from above; they emerge from below in the emotions and feelings of a people. "Christ the Liberator" is a symbolization emerging in Latin America. Ideas take a long time to become expressive symbols, but they do come. In the meantime, we live in an age of liturgical and symbolic transition which characterizes our discipleship.

Discipleship in our day requires on the one hand a patience with the long term changes required, and on the other hand a readiness to help make the Eucharist the sacrament of nourishment to the community. The community helps instruct the presider on how to preside better; the celebrant helps the community express their faith. A mutuality of help, cooperation, challenge, support, and honest critique can forge a vibrant community life.

It is the responsibility of everyone to help the liturgical life of the community grow. It is not the priest's problem but everyone's problem, because we are the Church at prayer. At this moment in history the Church is calling upon people to contribute their time and energy in new liturgical ways. Readers and lectors, ministers of the Eucharist, visitors who take communion to the sick, and other contributors offer a rich participation in the service of others. Without doubt, as is happening in countries throughout the world, even more participation through diverse roles in liturgy will be asked for from the community.

At the same time, we know that some people have been disaffected from liturgy during these decades. The reasons are many but perhaps there is less need to figure out the reasons than to join together in action. Praying together often breaks down barriers that talking together cannot remove. Perhaps we need to invite people to pray with us. That human support might be the nudge that is needed. Service to hurting and alienated members of the Church is too important a care for community to be overlooked.

It is also good to invite non-Catholics to services. Ignorance about one another, suspicion about some secret ritual, old stories of hideous practices, all are areas into which light could be shone. Nothing does this better than an experience of the joy of a community at prayer. Such an experience does not need to be explained, it communicates itself. Likewise, we might do well to visit non-Catholic services, especially if invited. Weddings and funerals are the most probable invitations, but other occasions are just as proper. It might be better to look upon such visits not as a lack of faith in one's own beliefs, but rather a sign of strength, integrity, and a willingness to learn from others about their practice of Christian faith. No one is asked to become less believing or participating in the community; on the contrary, people are invited to become more committed and loving of God and others.

A recent survey (by Andrew Greeley in the *Tablet* in late July of 1989) found that, while Catholic attendance at Sunday Eucharist was dropping in the United States, Catholics still attended Eucharist in the same overall numbers, just not as frequently. The average was once every three weeks. Thus Catholics still do attend Mass with regularity as an important expression in their lives. In the pre-Vatican Church, evening Masses were rare. The simple reason was that people had to fast from midnight if they wished to receive the Eucharistic Bread. With the changes in fasting laws, evening Masses became common and a whole new way of finding the rhythm of Mass in our lives became open to us. To attend Mass at 8 P.M. for a funeral and then at 7 A.M. the next morning for a daily Mass might put too much weight on attending and not on participating. Some can do it, others cannot. We are finding new ways to keep the Eucharist in our lives.

LIBERTY

Jesus gives us true freedom. The Spirit makes us free to be our most authentic selves. As Church, we have ways of organization, rules of proceeding, doctrines of belief, and principles for moral action. These are helps for our living discipleship. These helps require application according to the circumstances in which we find ourselves. At times we will not know how to apply them. In those circumstances, we might remember that we are the Church and must make the best decision that we can. The resources of the Church stand behind us in such instances, and our decision becomes one that the Church makes. Mistakes can and do occur. We cannot be afraid of making mistakes; rather, we should boldly do the Christlike act. Courage is a better guide than fear. To act in Christlike love is the one and only principle upon which we are judged. Hence we need tolerance for the diversity of responses which we make. Responsibility, commitment, authenticity before

God and others, honesty, and integrity are the virtues that we encourage in one another.

We might draw the line at the negatives of these virtues: lack of responsibility, no commitment, inauthenticity, dishonesty, and no integrity. At the same time, we must avoid judging others as if we possess the entire Holy Spirit of God. God alone judges love. For our part, we encourage people to those virtues which a Christlike love manifests. To hear the word of God in others inside and outside the Church, to encourage them to live love to its fullest, is the disciple's charge.

Hence, policies, whether in the Church or society or the world, that violate Christlike love are to be challenged as limiting the liberating love of God. Condemning others, whether in the Church or society or world, is not Christian love. When any soldier is killed, it cannot be a cause for rejoicing. Likewise, tragedies in other countries, AIDS, executions, and disasters are not occasions to rejoice. To be a disciple is to draw a line with oneself and with others in society to work for a loving world in true freedom.

PURSUIT OF HAPPINESS

The Church comes to others with a clear experience of being both sinner and saint. The Church has no fixed agenda but follows in discipleship the path God puts in front of us. We approve where possible, are not afraid of saying the truth, proclaim love of God and others even in the face of ridicule and death. For some, good news is bad news. People are challenged to give up their hatreds, jealousy, revenge, selfishness, and power trips. As the world changes, so do the ways of serving God in each changing circumstance. But this will always be the way of discipleship.

The Spirit of God dwells within every baptized Christian. This same Spirit dwells in the hearts of people throughout the world. We do not determine where God dwells. We are responsible for what we know from God, what God calls us to be, and how God works with us. We do not know the whole of God's reality; we only know a part.

The Zulus in South Africa have a beautiful saying: *Umuntu ngumuntu ngabantu,* "a person is a person through people." Our pursuit of happiness is tied to others. In the case of the Church, we recognize that our happiness comes from God and is shared with others, especially those who share the same Holy Spirit and therefore the same shared goal of happiness. We come alive in and through people at birth, depend on others throughout our lives, and enter into God's loving arms at death. We might amend the Zulu proverb slightly and say, "A disciple is a disciple through people." The identity of the Church might then be clearer.

The materialism of United States culture easily separates people into different income brackets depending on how much money they make. Happiness seems easily to slide into how much money you have and how much you can thereby buy. "Money can't buy happiness" is an American proverb because it is so easy to believe the opposite here. As disciples, we model a definite position towards happiness. Like the light on the mountain top, we shine forth for others. We do this by giving our time, our service, our self-renunciation, our reconciliation. We point to someone beyond ourselves that allows us to be persons to one another, not in competition or consumerism, but in the gift of ourselves. Chastity, celibacy, virginity, and sexual morality are meant to free us to make this self-donation without strings of consumerism attached.

Our own pursuit of happiness serves as a help to others to become the persons that they want to be. We become source and resource by living our own lives in transparency before others.

In summary, as Church we are nourished by the Lord and seek to nourish others in love. The Eucharist is the central act by which we symbolize who we are. A need exists to help clarify our Eucharistic presence to each other and to uncover the symbols that can express to each other and to others who we are. These symbols come neither quickly nor artificially by decree; they must be nurtured by the heart and accepted by the community.

Discipleship does not hold us back but turns us loose to love. The Church acts as a source and resource for us to live in this freedom of the Spirit. The dimensions of love are encouraged and their negatives discouraged in relations with people, society, and the world.

The happiness that comes from a life of love in God is something to be shared. Nothing is as contagious as love and happiness. For people who search for many types of happiness, we offer ours and invite others to find the person we have found. Our ways of loving represent a non-commercialized love that is freely given by the self, for others, in Christ.

Further Considerations

1. Personally: When do I most often experience myself as a member of a community of believers? What am I proud of in the Church? What am I ashamed of?

2. United States Context: What role could the Church play in shaping United States values and societal direction?

3. Global Context: What role could the Church play in shaping world-wide values and global direction?

4. Church Context: What do I think the Church will look like in the year 2100? What would I like it to look like?

Part III:

The Extension of Discipleship

The following two chapters are extensions of the themes of the Gospels and their practical applications. These two chapters can be read at any time, depending upon the background of the reader and his or her interest. The first chapter examines discipleship as spirituality in the modern world. The second chapter suggests ways to think about practical responses to the call of Jesus. Both offer important considerations about the implementation of our discipleship.

UNITED STATES DISCIPLESHIP AS SPIRITUALITY

I remember the story of the person who was asked if he had a spirituality. The punch line was "Yes: pray, pay, and obey." This joke has a sting of truth to it. Spirituality seemingly belongs to saints, mystics, and religious orders, not to the everyday believer. There is some truth to this because great mystics and saints, like Francis of Assisi, Dominic, Benedict, and Ignatius of Loyola, started religious orders.

The charisms of these founders became institutionalized in a group that represented the founder's unique view of the world. Other saints, like Teresa of Avila and Theresa of Liseaux and more recently Thomas Merton, although not founders, either reformed or contributed a new understanding of the original charisms. These religious orders, moreover, shared their respective spiritualities with others and so-called "third orders" of Franciscans and Dominicans emerged for lay people. The direction went one way: from religious communities to the everyday believers. Throughout the history of the Church these religious orders were called upon to continually share these approved spiritualities for the good of the Church. These spiritualities (Dominican, Franciscan, Benedictine, Ignatian, etc.) are a great tradition in our history and one we can all regard with pride.

But history also loses its memory, becomes selective, and overlooks facts. History's memory is as good as those who use it. We have forgotten that the institutionalization of the charism was not

163

the origin of it. These saints and mystics and founders of religious orders were first of all everyday believers who lived life in their worlds and responded to God's Spirit acting with and through them. The life of the Church is the soil from which these founders and their spiritualities emerged. It is important to observe that these individuals were astute observers of their life and times while, at the same time, deeply in love with God and aware of the truth of the gospel message. They managed to integrate message and world, translating the Word into a vision of life. That is spirituality.

Another important dynamic of spirituality was lost to memory, namely, that spiritualities remain intimately connected with the worlds from which they sprang. This forces two issues: (1) spiritualities must be able to transcend their own limited worlds and reach out to other worlds and times. For example, Franciscan spirituality, in order to live, must go beyond the world of Francis of Assisi where towns and cities were just beginning, to a modern world where megalopolises are taken for granted. (2) Spiritualities arose because of the need to live the gospel message in various times. For example, Dominic saw the need to preach to the masses of people the truth of God's word in the new Renaissance world that was developing. In some ways we can say that Dominic knew and used the developing mass medium of his day—preaching. Hence, spiritualities never meant withdrawing into the realm of the spirit, away from the body and its social situation. In a way, "spiritualities" is a partial description, because it isolates, and sometimes mistakenly emphasizes, the spirit over against the body and world. As indicated above, the founders provided many authentic ways of living in their cultural worlds.

The separation of spirit from body has been an unfortunate choice in the interpretation of spiritualities. Unintentionally, the realm of the spirit gradually ended up in the domain of religious communities. The "body side" became the temporal and was left to the domain of ethics. Hence, while religious communities were ruled by spiritualities, the everyday believer was ruled by morality. Indeed, the spirituality of the everyday believer was one of simple obedience.

With Vatican II, an interest in spirituality has emerged. The reasons for this are many, but the most central in my mind is the reintegration of gospel and life. The everyday believer is the Church and it is from this reservoir of faith that spiritualities take their strength. Religious orders serve the Church and thereby witness to the gospel message in a specialized way. Here is an image that might be of some help: think of the Church as a human body (an image favored since Paul). The organs—liver, heart, kidneys—represent specialized functions of the body, much as a religious order does within the Church. The organs are not separated from the blood, cells, and tissue on which the whole body depends; religious orders are not separated from the entire set of believers in the Church. First and foremost, the Church is the people who have entered into a faith relationship with God through Jesus. Religious orders take their shape precisely from the wider body of believers, never in contradistinction to them.

A reinterpretation of spiritualities as integrated with the world in which they began needs to be undertaken, although it is not this book's task. Our purpose remains to present an integrated spirituality of the everyday believer.

In defining spirituality, we must avoid overemphasizing the spirit from the totality of the person and his or her social relationships. We cannot use the image of a spider who spins webs from within itself. Spirituality is not living out of the core of ourselves as if it were independent from everything that makes us who we are. The spider web is self-enclosed system and not what a spirituality describes.

When we speak of the world, four environments must be distinguished: the individual, the family, society and institutions, and the rest of the natural world. These all reside together, penetrate each other, are tightly interwoven like a patchwork quilt, and remain distinct in their identities. For example, every person lives on the earth, but we live in different countries, do different organized tasks, come from a family, and exist as individuals. All four of these contexts will be present when we speak about the world.

The spirituality of the everyday believer must exist in four dimensions: inward, outward, backward, and forward (personal, social, past, and future). Integrating these four dimensions is the act of spirituality.

In what does the spirituality of discipleship consist when it is related to the modern world? Discipleship consists in the transformation of the self, society, and world, with the Word of God as the life source of this transformation. The Word of God provides life to the individual.

The Word of God finds us as people already immersed in culture. We have a history, language, institutions, society, values, and civilization that were given to us when we were born. Another way of saying this is that we are born in the middle of a human story. The nurturing matrix of this story is culture. Culture comes from the Latin word *colere* meaning "to till the soil." Culture stands for the achievements our history has managed. A helpful definition of culture is the symbolization of meaning and values. "Symbolization" indicates that every value is mediated and expressed through something else. For example, taking the fine arts as an example, a painter uses a canvas, a wall, a piece of wood, and watercolors, oils, or inks to paint a person or scene. A visual representation mediated through symbol takes place. Moving from fine arts to verbal communication, we see that this basis for socialization takes place always through language—English, French, German, Chinese, Spanish.

Languages are sounds which come to have accepted meanings. Grammar limits the way words are used, dictionaries specify common meanings and usages, and rules are followed. Language always symbolizes the human communicator. Not only language but also our labor, dwellings, furnishings, clothing, institutions, entertainment, and government symbolize meanings and values.

Culture is the product of human energy. The state of culture arrived at is known as civilization. For example, the United States lives in a technological society. Our stage of civilization becomes expressed in technology, unlike an industrial civilization or agricultural society.

One might think of this process of symbolization as an attempt to inculcate and cultivate what is human. Fine arts, for instance, express noble sentiments and emotions which educated people appreciate and take into themselves. There is good art and bad art. Classics are paintings or musical compositions or dances or sculptures that stand beyond their time and place to speak to something noble in us all. Beauty in this case cuts across cultures and sets standards for others to follow and improve upon if possible.

Whereas the fine arts are only one small area of life, the process of symbolization is the same with the entire world. Families, businesses, institutions, and forms of entertainment have a beauty of their own. Life itself becomes an art, attuned to history, society, and individual values that ennoble us.

The process of symbolization has many names. When a message enters into another culture and finds expression there, the process is called "inculturation." When a message is critically reappraised within the culture, it is called "reculturation." These words express well the process of reflecting on symbols in culture. From a Christological perspective, the word "incarnational" might be more helpful. To incarnate means literally "to make flesh" or "to enflesh." The greatest instance of incarnation is when God became flesh in Jesus. As Paul says, Jesus became the visible image of the invisible God. We would say that God symbolized God, that is, mediated who God is through the human form. To see Jesus is not to see the totality of God but only a part. This is what symbolization implies. The totality is hinted at only by particularization. The act of the incarnation implies a "making flesh" of human values and meaning. These symbols reach beyond the individual to various expressions that really are extensions of humanness. Just as our bodies, which are the symbols of ourselves, delimit the human world, so too an incarnational view delimits human values and meanings. Hence, culture is a process of incarnating human values in symbols.

The purpose of incarnation is not simply to be flesh but to become human. The word "humanization" is an adequate description. This process implies making the world we live in more and more humane. Because of our growing control over our many different environments, our ability to extend our values and meanings has increased. In a new way we can say that, for the first time on such a global scale, we possess the power to control our cultures. We know a great deal about nature, the laws of economics, society, and how to direct these powers for good or ill. That means we can direct them to enhance our humanization, or to do the opposite, which is dehumanization. For example, we contribute to another country's oppressive situation when we take their natural resources without true compensation. At one time this was considered shrewd business, now it is called oppression. Changes of consciousness occur. People want to be agents of their own destiny and refuse anything less. By fits and starts, trials and errors, we are arriving at a more global sense of humanization.

Humanization is a difficult concept to pin down. The reason rests on the many different interpretations of what "human" is. If the world could arrive at an agreed upon concept, then various cultures could work to symbolize it through their particular cultural values. The Chinese could do it this way, Africans that way, Americans another way. Ideally this would make for a wonderful world where everyone was trying to be truly human and could respect each other's efforts. If disagreement arose, a common ground would exist for understanding and perhaps resolving the problem.

However, such an ideal situation does not exist. It is easier to define the human by what we are not. For example, people generally agree that slavery is not humanizing, economic strangulation is not humanizing, famine and war are not humanizing, and all manners of threats, violence, and loss of freedom and education are not humanizing. Thus by working from the negative of humanization, we seem to have more concrete clues to what humanization can be. Even here there is a wide range of different voices.

For the Christian, humanization cannot stop with people becoming more able to control and improve their environment. The belief of the Christian includes salvation as the endpoint of humanization. The Christian believes that we are made for God, and that our relationship to one another includes both worshipping of God and relating to one another in ways that express who God tells us we are. In this case we are brothers and sisters to each other. The Christian vision of humanization therefore is a global community where people respect and love one another in familial ways. Justice, peace, reconciliation, and joy are qualities of this familial view. Salvation cannot be forced upon anyone; like discipleship, it is an invitation that allows many responses.

The following statements form a kind of checklist that provides rules for the process of incarnation of discipleship in a global humanity. They are "how to" rules that allow human communication that is attentive to the work of God's Holy Spirit already operating in the world. Their aim is to let God be a transforming participant in our world. In this sense they are conditions for discerning God's presence.

First, a new mental attitude is required of the disciple. We must all renounce any type of superiority complex and any monopoly on formal structures. The world has ceased to be markedly European for more than a century now and is fast losing its Western character. The division of the world into East and West is now changing to North and South.

Second, the disciple recognizes cultures and civilizations as potential bearers of Christian values. Christians should actively support these values even if they are incarnated in different ways than we are used to.

Third, a disciple must resist absolutizing his or her experience and with it cultural values. Such over-reacting to an unhappy past can occur, especially in new nations. The unhappy consequence would be an isolation from outside influences.

Fourth, a disciple should use interdisciplinary studies to understand a culture and avoid superficial, unbalanced, and subjective judgments. Profound and thorough studies are needed to bring what is possible to light.

Fifth, a disciple recognizes that the most intimate values can only be perceived within a culture itself. Those born into and living within a culture are the most inculturated. Hence, insertion into a culture is needed if we are to make correct judgments about culture. Likewise, people within a culture bear the heaviest burden of discerning what is genuine.

Sixth, a disciple recognizes the need for controlled experimentation, subject to evaluation and proceeding in stages. Because of the symbolizing importance of culture, manipulating and playing with culture will be destructive. Finding the right rhythm of incarnation requires reflecting upon experience.

Seventh, a disciple knows that he or she and the entire Church will feel at times challenged and at other times enriched by this process. The disciple will be changed by the process.

These seven conditions for discipleship in a modern, global humanity are not exhaustive, but they are identifiably necessary. Their purpose is to let God's truth, which is incarnated in ourselves and others, be manifested and placed at the disposal of others. At the same time, their purpose is to let God lead us into a community of peoples.

HOW TO THINK ABOUT OUR PRACTICAL RESPONSE TO JESUS

To live our response to Jesus in an American context is the goal of this book. I have attempted to present the scriptural understanding of Jesus, the present day meaning of the Jesus Event, and some implications for practical living out of discipleship. Our response cannot be that of people of the first century; we are people of the twentieth century moving towards the twenty-first.

Too often one way of responding becomes the only way of responding. For instance, I know families who commit themselves once a month to serve lunch in a downtown soup kitchen. While this response is important and nourishing to the spirituality of these people individually and as a family, for me to do the same is not the point. The danger becomes my identification of a wonderfully charitable work with what I should do. The Lord may be asking me to respond in other areas, to other people, in other ways. The example of many people's response to discipleship is just that: an example from which I might like to follow or which teaches me new ways of finding out how I am to respond.

Let us consider the difference between unity and uniformity. A uniform that one wears to school or puts on before an athletic event is an identifiable article of clothing. Everyone looks the same. Sometimes "looking the same" adds a sense of corporate identity or solidarity; "We are on the same team." That everyone looks the same, however, does not necessarily mean that people are the same, think the same, feel the same, or have anything in common other than appearance.

170

Unity means oneness. Unity implies that bonding exists on some level. If we look at school uniforms, we can say that a unity exists, namely that these students attend the same school. If we use personal relationships as the criterion of bonding, then we do not know if a unity exists. There is no evidence that people who wear the same school uniform even talk to one another, let alone respect one another and build up personal relationships. Of course I am using the strict logical interpretation because we know that some human bonding does take place at every school. But the point is that uniformity and unity are not necessarily identical.

When speaking about our discipleship, the source of unity is the Holy Spirit poured over each one of us in baptism. The Holy Spirit also becomes the criterion of unity. As the early Church realized and struggled with itself, identifying the presence of the Holy Spirit was crucial. Paul, more than any other of the New Testament writers, labored to help the fledgling Christian communities grow in their knowledge of the Spirit. Paul pointed to the charisms, or gifts, of the spirit. He also showed Christians how to test the presence of the Spirit by the effects of the relationship between the disciple and the Spirit. The "gifts of the Holy Spirit" and the "fruits of the Holy Spirit" that we perhaps learned in catechism class were extremely vital to Paul's early churches. They also have been important to other churches, down through the centuries.

We have also relied on other criteria. One has been fidelity to the Magisterium of the entire Church, expressed in the bishops and the pope. One might call this obedience or fidelity to authority. In the early churches and outside the Pauline churches, this reliance upon authority in testing the Spirit's presence still measured the effects of the Spirit. The authority involved recognized the Spirit and helped the people to know which gifts were being recognized and used. We might call this the administering of the affairs of the communities. But the authority invested by the people in the recognition of the gifts was never to substitute for the gifts themselves. A uniformity of procedure, we might say, never was to substitute for the unity of the Spirit.

Hence, the unity that we share is that of the Spirit. We need administering of the gifts at certain times and places so that the proper gifts lead the whole people closer to God. As Paul wrestled to realize, not all the gifts of the Spirit are to be used at one and the same time. In the liturgy, for example, Paul arranged a hierarchy of gifts to be used which was determined by the gift's contribution to the greatest service of all. Thus, speaking in tongues which could not be interpreted in the worshipping community should give way to the gift of preaching by which all derived a greater closeness to the Spirit. But Paul was not denigrating any gift by acknowledging a hierarchy of gifts; he simply presented the context as important to the organizing of the gifts. Presumably, Paul would present another hierarchy in a different circumstance.

Therefore we need on the one hand to encourage people to respond to the Spirit in their discipleship, and on the other hand to contribute their gifts to the service of others, which might call for some uniformity for the sake of the wider community. This working principle flows from discipleship itself, recognizing the reality that our discipleship is one with the people of God everywhere throughout the world and at the same time relies on our response to the Spirit. Thus the disciple lives his or her spirituality mindful of the two poles between which the people of God live: unity and uniformity. One never becomes the other but they remain in interaction.

A second consideration might be helpful to represent the desired two-fold relationship of unity and diversity as we live out discipleship. The challenge for both the individual and the community is to hold to a unity of the Spirit and to make room for a variety of responses.

Although not perfect, a quantitative example of a bar graph can demonstrate how we all bring different gifts before the Lord, with different challenges and different graces. We drew graphs in school and now we see them every day in newspapers and magazines. The graph is a rectangle and each bar represents one item. The filling in of the bar goes from least to highest along the vertical side. Each new bar moves along the horizontal side. In a completed graph we see a row of darkened bars of varying heights. The result is an overall display of information that we might not otherwise possess.

Now imagine that at baptism every disciple becomes a bar graph. Each bar represents a virtue, such as love, generosity, compassion, forgiveness, prudence, wisdom, kindness, justice, chastity, fortitude, and so on. Depending upon the strength of my virtue, the bar is higher or lower. Every person's bar graph would be different. For some, depending upon personality and other factors such as family, love might be easy and that bar very high. For others, perhaps due to a parent who did not love them or to other bad experiences, love is difficult and the bar low. For the loving person, to love may be easy. For one who has not known love, to love even a little might be heroic. Therefore, just because one's virtue or bar is high, it is not a sign of heroic discipleship. We are all different.

Our bar graph does help us to point out that talents, in the manner of the virtues listed here, vary a great deal. What is easy for one person might be difficult for another. Placing the bars side by side indicates that every person brings a number of other virtues into play with love. For example, the person who has been hurt, let's say sexually abused as a child, and finds it difficult to love might possess a tremendous virtue of compassion for others. On the other hand, the person who found it easy to love might become frustrated when compassion for strangers is called for. The point is that no two people are the same and each person brings a variety of virtues, all at different strengths, to his or her discipleship. We can expect, therefore, that the response to the Lord may come in different varieties. The most important reality, one that is sometimes overlooked, is that we have a bar graph at all! The presence of the bar graph indicates that we are baptized Christians in discipleship, the minimum that makes us all equal. How we live our baptism, according to our responses to the Lord's ways, varies as we bring different and developing gifts to the service of the Lord.

While the dangers of using a quantitative image are clear, it serves the purpose of showing the complex number of virtues that make up our lives. No two of us are the same and so my own response might differ from the response of others. I need not worry that something is missing in me, or that I am not measuring up to someone else's chart. To be faithful to the Lord in the disciple's path that I am on is my unique challenge.

My concern comes from my own and others' exasperation over the quest to be like people we admire and to perform actions that we admire. We are blessed to have examples of discipleship like Mother Teresa in Calcutta. She lives by one simple Christian virtue: to help those who are dying. She measures her love by Jesus' own command to care for the neighbor, and so she goes to the poorest of the poor who have no one to care for them. She does not try to baptize, evangelize, or demand that governments intervene to prevent this outrage to humanity. She just goes on caring for the dying in whatever way she can and in whatever way they ask. That is all she does. And this simple, Christian disciple has thereby touched the heart of nations throughout the world. She has been given many humanitarian awards of great distinction and is one of the most admired women in the world.

I would like to be like her. Others have told me that they would too. Many people are coming to join in her work and her work is spreading throughout the world. This is good. Should I go? When asked the same question a few years ago by some Americans, she told them to stay in America and work with the poorest of the poor. Her response was quite insightful, she continued and said that she found the United States people to be some of the loneliest in the world. She knew what to do in Calcutta, but not in New York. She suggested that the need was greater and different in our own cities. Her statement is a lesson for every disciple.

Some people have a great sensitivity to justice, perhaps stemming from a great virtue in their personalities and developed through exposure to injustice. I am not like that, nor do I have this personal quality. My reaction is not to abandon justice, that would be un-Christian and sinful, but to find out how I can contribute to the justice of humanity. For one it might mean lobbying in Washington, for another it might mean hours given freely to organizations, for others it might mean binding the wounds of the hurting. There are many ways to do justice. Everyone can make a contribution and we are all called to do so by the nature of the gospel message itself. But justice has many dimensions and requires many people's efforts in many areas. Causes of injustice can be agreed upon, but even here the resistance is multiple. Injustice has legal, historical, personal, economic, political, fearful, selfish, ignorant, and power-hungry dimensions. We can all find the ways that we can most effectively combat injustice, according to our own discipleship.

Injustice, however, is not the only opposition to the kingdom of God. We can multiply the obstacles of hatred, violence, selfishness, fear, and so on. While working against injustice, my discipleship might come in a response to other areas. My own sensitivities and talents might best be applied more directly in other areas. That is good. Thus we need a wide range of responses, with the latitude and freedom to respond wherever we find God inviting us. At the same time, we cannot become individuals separated from other Christians. We do not want to either dampen the Spirit or compete with its graces. We need each other's discerning of the Spirit in our midst. Open to the Spirit, our efforts will be unified. It is the same one Spirit we all are listening and responding to. For in the last analysis, the unity we seek is from God. In the end, just as a practical Christology serves a living discipleship, so too does a living discipleship serve a practical Christology.